New Directions for Children's Ministries

New Directions for Children's Ministries

by
Miriam J. Hall

Beacon Hill Press of Kansas City
Kansas City, Missouri

Copyright 1980
Beacon Hill Press of Kansas City

ISBN: 0-8341-0639-6

Printed in the
United States of America

Dedicated to my much-loved daughter,

Amy Beth.

She brings sunshine and joy into my life,
reminds me of the importance of
children's ministry, and
patiently lives with a mother who both
travels and writes books.

Contents

Foreword

Born in the crucible of personal experience is the exciting message of this book. The author has committed her very life to effect a "ministry to children."

Miriam Hall is a gifted teacher and trained educator. Growing up in the church, she served in every imaginable leadership position—including teaching children and leading children's workers as director of children's ministries on a local church staff. Her local church involvement has been reinforced by a parallel involvement as a public school teacher and as administrator of a massive public school reading program in Denver, Colo. No person I know is more qualified to address this subject.

New Directions for Children's Ministries is just that. It is a fresh and contemporary picture of the world of the child. Beginning with a solid biblical base for creating ministries to meet the needs of children, the book proceeds to detail a variety of ways in which such ministry can be realized. It addresses the whole spectrum of ministries to children that may be programmed through the local church. Directors of children's ministries will discover this book to be a "gold mine." Teachers of children's classes will discover some wonderful new directions. Pastors, parents, and students will benefit from the unique insights of one whose whole life has been absorbed with children.

As you read the intriguing discussion of "Meeting the Needs of Children" or "Leading a Child to Christ," you will become aware that this writer has been there and knows firsthand about those of whom she writes. Without reservation, I recommend this book to you. May God use it as a significant and enjoyable part of your equipping for service.

RICHARD SPINDLE

Preface

Any change in organizational structure and procedure leads to questions from those who are responsible for implementing the change. Since the General Assembly of 1976 formed the Department of Children's Ministries, as a part of the Division of Christian Life, questions have been coming to the department. Most of these have come from Board of Christian Life chairmen and directors of children's ministries, both at the district and the local levels.

These questions have been dealt with through letters, articles, workshops, and other means, but the need persists for a book which explains the specific responsibilities of the Department of Children's Ministries and its relationship to the rest of the Division of Christian Life. *New Directions for Children's Ministries* has been written to meet that need.

Exploration of what total ministry to children means is the framework on which this book is built. What kinds of ministries are available to the church? What contribution does each one make to the life of the child? How does the church organize to provide total ministry for its children? What workers and equipment are needed? As you read these pages, you will find answers for these questions and many more. Every effort has been made to try to look at children's ministries from the viewpoint of those who are involved in this area of the church's task. Detailed job descriptions are given; organizational charts are pictured; techniques for working with children are discussed. Every church, whatever its size, will find helpful ideas to use in developing its children's ministries.

New Directions for Children's Ministries is designed to be a text for those who have responsibility for ministering to children. It is not a book to be skimmed through lightly; it needs to be studied. If you use the book as it has been designed, you will find in it the blueprint for an effective, total ministry to the children in your church.

ROBERT D. TROUTMAN
Editorial Director
Department of Children's Ministries

Acknowledgments

I'm indebted to several people who helped me in various ways as I wrote this book. I'd like to express my appreciation to them. Thanks to:

—Donna Fillmore and Mark A. York for sharing with me information from their writings for use in Chapters 5 and 10.

—The Department of Children's Ministries staff for their support and input concerning the various ministries.

—Pam Stelting for her typing and retyping of the manuscript.

A special thanks to Robert D. Troutman for the excellent and thoughtful way he edited the book.

MIRIAM J. HALL

*Every child comes with the
message that God is not yet
discouraged with man.*
                    TAGORE

1

Who Needs
Children's Ministry?

"A Denver teacher-researcher reports at least 84% of fifth-graders surveyed said they had tried alcohol at least once. Never did fewer than 50% say they hadn't tried it at least ten times. Teachers in middle-class, white, suburban areas called alcoholism a 'Lion Outside the Door,' and warned workshop attendants to expect major problems in years ahead, as families with both parents working produce children who decide to 'drink their breakfasts.' The same study revealed that 6-9% of sixth-graders have 'experienced sex.'"[1]

"Homosexual life-styles will soon be studied in San Francisco public schools as part of the education curriculum. The measure was approved 7-0 by the city school board."[2]

"An authority in occultism declares, 'It is our aim to get a witch in every elementary school in the U.S.A.'"[3]

Facts like these show us that children in today's society are receiving more—and at the same time less—attention than ever before. On the one hand, they are the objects of close scrutiny by just about everyone from the president to the manufacturers of breakfast cereal. On the other, there are serious indications that many of the deeper needs of children are being terribly neglected.

Areas of Attention to Children

1. Without doubt, children are receiving more *material* benefits than in times past. In our consumer-oriented society, advertisers have discovered that the way to sell new products to parents is through their children. They spend billions of dollars every year appealing to the interests and desires of the young. The number and variety of books, magazines, clothes, and toys for children increases daily. Not only are parents more and more willing to give these items to their children, but they are providing them with greater amounts of money of their own. Thus, the number of things the child is able to buy for himself is increasing.

2. Recent studies have emphasized the basic needs of children as human beings. We now know that the *emotional* environment of the child is just as important as the physical care he receives. In order for a child to grow up healthy and happy, he needs to have a sense of self-worth. Parents and teachers are being urged to take the feelings of children seriously, to emphasize the child's unique abilities, and to let him know that he is important to those around him.

3. Closely related to this, emphasis on the *"rights"* of children has become a growing concern of many groups and organizations. In the face of increasing overpopulation, child abuse, and poverty, these people have launched campaigns to see that children around the world have enough to eat and wear and that they receive proper health care. Some are even promoting the concept that children have legal rights and may challenge their parents' authority in the areas of discipline and religious preference.

4. The *education* of children is a multimillion-dollar industry. Educators cannot decide what should be taught, or how. They wrestle back and forth with the issues of "progressive education" or "back to basics." All agree that children need to be educated, and that this goal is worthy of time, personnel, buildings, and money. New books on how to make the educational process palatable, both to children and their teachers, appear on the market every day.

All of these trends, some of which are good, point to the fact that increased attention is being given to children today.

But unfortunately, there are just as many signs that in several crucial areas the deep needs of children are being neglected.

Areas of Neglect of Children

Children need love and personal attention; but far too many are not receiving it in the quantities they should have. Why is this? There are *several influencing factors.*

1. The rate of *divorce* has more than doubled during the last 12 years. It has risen more than 700 percent in the last century. As homes break up, children lose the benefit of a resident father or mother. The remaining parent, who usually must work, has less time and energy to devote to active, growing children, who are going through trauma as a result of the divorce. Loyalty to both parents causes confusion and builds feelings of anger, frustration, guilt, resentment, hopelessness, rejection, and insecurity.

An alarming result of all this is child suicide. The child is trying to get "back at someone" and is trying to call attention to a desperate situation. When he doesn't get that attention, he becomes depressed, which is an important signal of suicide. Psychiatrists did not even recognize depression in children until about 10 years ago.[4]

2. Even in stable two-parent families the *mother often works* outside the home. As a result, many preschoolers spend considerable time in the care of a baby-sitter or at a day-care center. This is not always all bad; but if the mother is harried with household tasks when she returns from work, she may not take the time for her children that they need and want.

3. As young parents find themselves unable to cope with the pressures of today's society and the demands made upon them, *child abuse* is increasing. This problem affects both the children of low-income families and those from middle- and high-income groups.

4. Another trend which seriously affects children is *mobility.* In previous generations it was not unusual for a child to grow to adulthood not only in the same town, but often in the same house. He was surrounded by relatives, friends, and neighbors who had also been there as long as he could remember. Today, almost a fourth of the population in the U.S. moves

each year. Only a few families stay in the same house for 10 years or more.

Such constant moving affects the stability of family life. The child is separated from the extended family of grandparents, aunts, uncles, and cousins. He cannot establish roots because close relationships have little time to develop. Instead, he is constantly forced to make new friends and to adjust to a new school and community.

The effects of this are seen dramatically in the life of a small boy who seemed sick. "Repeated examinations by a medical doctor failed to reveal any reasons for the illness. After many months the boy confessed to his parents, 'I was afraid you would move again while I was at school.'"[5]

5. Children need discipline—consistent training in what is right and wrong. Unfortunately, *permissive theories of child-rearing* have left many parents unsure about what to do and when. Absentee fathers have often turned over this job to their wives, who may or may not be able to cope with the responsibility. As a result, the whims of the child become law, and he gradually becomes a tyrant who threatens his parents more each year.

6. Children need protection from the evils of the world; but today's children are *exposed to doses of sex, violence, and profanity*. They see it on television, hear it on the radio, and observe it in the lives of adults who have abandoned the traditional values which were once commonly held even by non-Christians. The typical American home has the television set turned on six hours and 14 minutes each day. During this time, children are not only being exposed to sex and violence, but their values are also being shaped in other areas. The TV emphasizes beauty, money, intelligence, and brawn as channels for attaining worth. Children develop inferiority feelings when they sense they cannot measure up to the television standard.

7. So the *formation of values* has become a problem, too. This is ironic in a day when so much is being said about value clarification. The problem is that in many cases children are being taught only the process of value formation. They are told that it does not matter what you believe as long as you know what it is and how you arrived at the value. As traditional values such as trust in God, honesty, truthfulness, and hard work are being called into question and abandoned by many,

children are being left with no clear foundation upon which to build their lives.

8. Children need an opportunity to be children—yet even this is being denied many. The emphasis in today's society is on *growing up as rapidly as possible.* Look at children. They can no longer be recognized by their clothing. Other than its size, one can hardly distinguish the child's garment from that of his parent. Many children's toys, such as Ken and Barbie dolls, suggest to boys and girls that being a child is not good, that he should hurry on to the teen years and teen activities.

The sad thing about this is that often parents are active participants in the destruction of childhood. They do ridiculous things. Three-year-olds receive electric trains. Five-year-olds are dressed in caps and gowns for kindergarten graduation. Little girls who would like to play with dolls are taken to studios to learn to dance. In baseball children are expected to perform as professionals—before they have hips big enough to hold up their uniforms or hands big enough to grasp the ball. We push them to read while they still prefer to stack blocks.[6]

Parents are more concerned with what the children will become—adults—rather than what they are now—children. The noisiness and nonsense of childhood are disliked. Teachers, too, want children to sit down and be quiet, to produce, to conform, to be mini-adults. Pushing a child into adult behavior does not help him become an adult. It only frustrates him and causes him to be bored with life at an early age. Many children have experienced "everything" at age 15, so they are forced to experiment with drugs, alcohol, and sex in order to relieve boredom and find excitement in life.

What does all of this say to the church as we try to answer the question "Who needs children's ministry?" It tells us that there are at least three groups of people to whom we must reach out.

First, children need children's ministry. Today, more than ever before, children need the attention, love, and help of concerned Christians who understand their deepest needs and who want to help boys and girls experience the quality of life God intended for them to have.

Second, parents need children's ministry. A "trouble so deep and pervasive as to threaten the future of our nation" has gripped the U.S.A., according to documents drawn up at the

White House Conference on Children, late in 1970. That trouble is "national neglect of children and those primarily engaged in their care—America's parents." Dr. Urie Bronfenbrenner, chairman of the conference, said, "The actual patterns of life in America today are such that children and families come last." Our society requires its citizens first of all to meet the demands of their jobs and then to fulfill civic and social obligations.[7]

In the midst of all the confusion they face today, parents need spiritual guidance for themselves so they can, with God's help, be the example their children need. They also need help from the church in knowing how to provide adequate spiritual direction for their children.

Last of all, the church needs children's ministry. If the children of today do not have their needs met—if they do not come to a saving knowledge of Jesus Christ and learn how to live and grow in Him—from whence will the church of tomorrow come? It is true that some people are saved as adults; but many of today's adult Christians were saved as children, or at least influenced to make an adult decision by the spiritual training they received as children. If the church is to continue to "go . . . into all the world, and preach the gospel" (Mark 16:15, KJV), it will need strong groups of adults who were nurtured in the Lord as children. It is safe to say that only if the church continues to minister effectively to children will there be a strong church of the future.

This book is designed to help children's leaders of the church to: (1) catch a vision of the importance of our task; and (2) learn how to minister effectively to children. Two thousand years ago Jesus' disciples wanted to turn away children in order to have more time for adults. Jesus said, "Let the little children come to me, and do not hinder them" (Mark 10:14). Today His words shine like a light through the ages, beckoning us to join Him in one of the most important works in the world—ministering to children.

REFERENCE NOTES

1. From the Religious News Service as published in *Ministry* magazine, January 1978.

2. Taken from the monthly publication, *The Church Around the World,* Tyndale House Publishers, Wheaton, Ill.

3. From the Child Evangelism Fellowship New Jersey newsletter.

5. John M. Drescher, *Seven Things Children Need* (Scottdale, Pa.: Herald Press, 1976), p. 37.

4. "Children's Suicide Rate Shows Big Increase," *San Diego Union* (Dec. 12, 1976), cited in Barbara Bolton and Charles T. Smith, *Creative Bible Learning* (Glendale, Calif.: Regal Books, 1977), p. 24.

6. *Ibid.*, pp. 23-24.

7. Urie Bronfenbrenner, et al., "And the Last Shall Be First," reprint of Forum 15, Children and Parents Together in the World, White House committee document, p. 1, cited in Roy B. Zuck and Robert E. Clark, eds., *Childhood Education in the Church* (Chicago: Moody Press, 1975), p. 9.

2

*Religious words have value to
the child only as his experience
in the home gives them meaning.*
CANON LUMB

A Biblical Look at Children's Ministry

The Bible is not a manual on the care and training of children; nor did Sunday school and similar organizations for children exist when it was written. But the Scriptures do have some interesting insights into (1) characteristics of children and what our attitude toward the child should be; (2) the need for religious instruction of children; and (3) methods for effectively teaching and ministering to children.

The Nature and Characteristics of Children

"Sons are a heritage from the Lord, children a reward from him" (Ps. 127:3).

"A woman giving birth to a child has pain because her time has come; but when her baby is born she forgets the anguish because of her joy that a child is born into the world" (John 16:21).

"This is what the Lord Almighty says: 'Once again men and women of ripe old age will sit in the streets of Jerusalem . . . The city streets will be filled with boys and girls playing there'" (Zech. 8:4-5).

"Folly is bound up in the heart of a child, but the rod of discipline will drive it far from him" (Prov. 22:15).

"Even a child is known by his actions, by whether his conduct is pure and right" (Prov. 20:11).

"No nation has ever set the child in the midst more deliberately than the Jews did. . . . It was Rabbi Judah the Holy who uttered the famous saying, 'The world exists only by the breath of school children.'"[1] In Jewish families children were considered a highly prized gift from God. The birth of a boy was considered an especially great honor because it brought with it the possibility that perhaps that child would be the promised Messiah. When a baby was about to be born, friends, relatives, and local musicians gathered at the home. If the baby was a boy, the group hailed the event with singing, music, and congratulations.

The *name* the parents gave to the child often reflected their joy. For example, Saul and Samuel both mean "asked for." The stories of Rebekah, Rachel, and Hannah emphasize the fact that childlessness was a fate almost too awful to be borne. The Jewish rabbis said that seven types of people were excommunicated from God; and the list began, "A Jew who has no wife or a Jew who has a wife and who has no child." Childlessness was a valid ground for divorce.

The *quality of life* experienced by Jewish children was much better than that of children in other societies. The story of Baby Moses illustrates the way children were treasured and protected even in times of crisis. Later, when the Law was given, safeguards for child welfare were included. Child sacrifice, widely practiced in other cultures, was prohibited (Lev. 18:21). Fathers were to treat even the children of less-favored wives fairly (Deut. 21:15-17), and kindness to orphans was stressed (24:17-22). Children could not be punished for the wrongdoing of their parents (v. 16). New Testament writings went a step further and admonished parents not to discipline so harshly that they discouraged or embittered their children (Eph. 6:4 and Col. 3:21).

It is important to notice, however, that while children were important, Jewish society was not a child-centered society in the same sense that many Western countries are today. Women and children were considered less important than adult males (notice the way these groups were listed in the story of the feeding of the 5,000). The Bible speaks frequently of the obligation of parents to love and provide for children, but nothing about the "rights" of children to expect or demand these things. Children were to be subservient to parents, respectful and obedient (Exod. 20:12; Col. 3:20).

Insights into child characteristics are also reflected in the Scriptures. Both Zechariah and Jesus referred to children at play. Jesus even mentioned the disagreements that so often arise in childish play. In other references, children are pictured as dependent, trusting, foolish, in need of firm discipline, and sometimes wayward. Like everyone else in the human race, children are sinners who, if left to their own devices, pursue a pathway of wrongdoing (Prov. 22:15; 29:15; Rom. 3:23).

Jesus' attitude toward children reflected the prevailing opinions of His society, but it also differed sharply in some respects. When we look at the Bible stories about Jesus and children, it is easy to see that He placed high value upon them and upon meeting their needs. This is shown (1) by His reaction when He was asked to help a child; (2) by the ways He interacted with children; (3) by the things He said about them.

1. Jesus was always ready to interrupt His ministry to adults, or His own personal plans, to meet the needs of a child. In the story of Jairus' daughter, Jesus was busy teaching adults when the distraught father arrived with his request. Jairus asked that Jesus come to his house and lay His hands on his daughter. All three Gospel accounts indicate that Jesus immediately stopped what He was doing and went with Jairus.

In the story of the epileptic boy, Jesus had just come down from the Mount of Transfiguration—perhaps the greatest scene of glory He experienced during His life on earth. However, He quickly laid aside even the lingering recollections of that glory in order to meet the needs of a child.

2. Jesus' interaction with children also reflects His high regard for them. When He addressed Jairus' daughter, He used the Aramaic expression, *"Talitha Koum,"* which means literally, "Little lamb, I say unto thee, arise."[2] Another small detail shows His consideration for the needs of a child. Immediately after the girl had been raised, Jesus commanded her parents to give her something to eat. G. Campbell Morgan makes this comment about the action: "We talk about the *Man* Jesus, and blessed be His humanity; but this is God, and He robs death of its prey and thinks about the meal of a little maiden."[3]

Toward the end of His life, as Jesus was on His way to Jerusalem for the last time, mothers brought their children to Him to be blessed. The disciples' motive for trying to send the mothers and children away was probably true concern for Jesus. They knew He was overworked and burdened by His coming passion and death. But Jesus' reaction to their act was one of indignation. Not only did He tell His followers not to hinder the children from coming, but He took time to lift each one into His arms and bless him.

3. The most explicit evidence of Jesus' attitude toward children can be discovered in His statements about them. In these statements, He showed *why* children are important, and *how* very important they are.

The incident of the child in the midst arose out of an argument the disciples were having over which of them would be greatest in God's kingdom. Instead of answering their petty question directly, Jesus called a little child to Him and, with His arms around the child, made these startling statements: "Unless you change and become like little children, you will never enter the kingdom of heaven. . . . whoever humbles himself like this child is the greatest in the kingdom of heaven. And whoever welcomes a little child like this in my name welcomes me" (Matt. 18:3-5). To this last statement Mark adds, "Whoever welcomes me does not welcome me but the one who sent me" (9:37). Matthew rounds out the statements with, "See that you do not look down on one of these little ones. For I tell you that their angels in heaven always see the face of my Father in heaven" (18:10).

Perhaps to impress these facts upon His disciples, who apparently had missed the point altogether, Jesus added these words when He later blessed the children: "The kingdom of God belongs to such as these" (Luke 18:16).

Jesus considered children to be so important because He realized how much God, His Father, values them. The Jews at that time believed that every child had a guardian angel. They were also familiar with the concept of a king and his court officials. Only the most important of those officials had direct access to the king. Jesus was saying, in effect, that children are so important their guardian angels can come into the presence of God at all times. He was willing to give complete attention to the care of the child.

4. Perhaps another reason Jesus was so ready to minister to children was that He realized it was one way to reach their parents. Three interesting instances of this are recorded in the New Testament—in the stories of Jairus, the Syro-Phoenician woman, and the nobleman.

When we take a good look at these parents, we discover that their coming to Jesus at all was remarkable. Jairus was the ruler of the synagogue. This means that he was the administrative head of the synagogue and was responsible for the conduct of the services. By virtue of his position, he was one of the most important people in the community. At the time Jairus came to Jesus, most of these rulers were definitely opposed to Jesus' work. Those who were not kept aloof from Him to avoid pressure from their associates.

The woman from Syrian Phoenicia was also an unlikely candidate to appeal to Jesus for help. She came from Canaanite territory where the people were longstanding enemies of the Jews. Some think she was a worshiper of Astarte.

The nobleman also had some things to overcome in seeking help from Jesus. He had to travel about 20 miles from Capernaum to Cana to even get to Jesus. Also, he was a man of high rank in Herod's court. No doubt in coming to Jesus he risked derision, if not downright persecution.

Probably none of these people would have sought out Jesus under ordinary circumstances; but in their fear for the lives of their children, they forgot about religious differences, social standing, and popular opinion. What impact did Jesus' ministry to their children have upon these parents? It is difficult to say for sure in the case of Jairus. However, the story of the miracle spread rapidly throughout the region, and Jairus might have had a hand in this. In the cases of the woman and the nobleman, there is rather clear evidence of conversion. Barclay points out that when the woman first came to Jesus, she called Him by His popular, political title, "Son of David." But in the end, she called Him "Lord."[4] John states that the nobleman "and all his household believed" (John 4:53).

All of this says to us that working with children is not a second-rate task. In fact, if the reverse of Jesus' statements about children is true, then to reject a child is to reject Christ— and God as well. But what should be the nature of our work with children? What can they learn about God, and when should this instruction begin? The Bible also gives us some very definite clues about this.

Biblical Guidelines for Religious Education of Children

"On that day tell your son, 'I do this because of what the Lord did for me when I came out of Egypt'" (Exod. 13:8).

"These commandments that I give you today are to be upon your hearts. Impress them on your children. Talk about them when you sit at home and when you walk along the road, when you lie down and when you get up. Tie them as symbols on your hands and bind them on your foreheads. Write them on the doorframes of your houses and on your gates" (Deut. 6:6-9).

"In the future, when your children ask you, 'What do these stones mean?' tell them . . ." (Josh. 4:6-7).

"Train a child in the way he should go, and when he is old he will not turn from it" (Prov. 22:6).

"Fathers, do not exasperate your children; instead, bring them up in the training and instruction of the Lord" (Eph. 6:4).

When we read verses like these, it becomes more than clear that God intended for children to have religious instruction. They are to learn about His acts in behalf of people and about the laws He has given. Through the frequency and repetition of instruction, their lives literally are to be saturated with knowledge of God.

The Jewish system of education for children was *based on commandments from God;* and the result was a totally religious education. Even later in Jewish history when public synagogue schools were organized, the purpose of those schools was to teach the Law of God. Because of their understanding of themselves as God's people, the Jews had no interest in what would not be termed a liberal education. They were the people whom God— who is holy—had called apart to be holy as well. Their lives were to be different from those around them as their knowledge of God resulted in righteous living.

The Jewish concept of education was intensely *life-related.* Josephus said:

> There are two ways of coming at any sort of learning, and a moral conduct of life: the one is by instruction in words, the other by practical exercises. Now, other law-givers (that is, other than Moses) have separated these two

ways in their opinions, and choosing one of those ways of instruction, or that which best pleased every one of them, neglected the other. Thus did the Lacedaimonians and the Cretans teach by practical exercises, but not by words; while the Athenians, and almost all the other Grecians, made laws about what was to be done, or left undone, but had no regard to the exercising thereto in practice.[5]

The basis of the Jewish opinion was their understanding that *knowledge* included much more than just intellectual understanding. The word for *wisdom,* usually translated "instruction" in Proverbs, meant the ability to understand the difference between good and evil and the application of this understanding to life. The wise man pictured in Proverbs was prudent, friendly, temperate, chaste, diligent, truthful, kind to the poor, and even to enemies. He was a success in life because he lived by God's principles.

Based on these understandings, certain *principles and practices* in educating children began to emerge. The Jews felt that (1) education of children was imperative; (2) that it was the responsibility of parents; (3) that it should permeate all of life; (4) that it should begin early; and (5) that it should be accomplished through a variety of methods in different places and at various times. Thus, as we look at the Jewish educational system, we receive clues about the kind of training they felt children should have, the scope and setting of that education, and effective methods of teaching.

The Scriptures in Deuteronomy make it clear that the education of children was a must, that it was the responsibility of parents, and that it was to be related to all aspects of life. This attitude is also reflected in Jewish writings. Josephus said, "We take the most pains of all with the instruction of children, and esteem the observation of the laws, and the piety corresponding with them, the most important affair of our whole life."[6] According to tradition, one famous rabbi would not even eat breakfast until he had escorted his son to school. And it was said that the Jews would rather interrupt the building of the Temple than to interrupt school.

Not only did the Jews feel that religious education was a must, but they also felt it should begin early. One rabbi, in talking about the education of children, said that teaching a child early could be compared to writing on a clean sheet of paper. A late beginning is like writing on soiled paper. A comment in the Talmud reads, "If we do not keep our children to religion when they are young, we shall certainly not be able to do so in later years."

Before the Exile, the education of the child was carried out entirely at home by his parents. The father, as the head of the home, was responsible for this education; but the mother was also important (Prov. 1:8; 6:20). During the period of the Exile, synagogue schools were formed. Nevertheless, responsibility for the child's education remained with the parents and still centered largely in the home. There religion and life intertwined in such a way that they could not be separated. The child was saturated with his religious education.

As soon as a child could speak—around age three—he was helped to memorize the Shema, the affirmation of faith found in Deut. 6:4. But even before this, he took part in the religious ceremonies which occurred at home. As we can see from the various scriptures about childhood education, many of these ceremonies were designed to arouse a child's curiosity and lead him to ask questions.

One of these ceremonies which even a young child would notice involved the mezuzah. This was a small wooden box fastened to the doorpost of the home. Inside were parchments with the words of the Shema printed on them. Each time a person entered or left the home, he reached up, touched the box with his finger, kissed his finger, and repeated a benediction.

Also at about age three, it was recommended that the child be taken to the synagogue service. Under the leadership of his parents, he was taught to begin observing the Sabbath. At a little older age, he was encouraged to fast at least part of the day on the Day of Atonement. Boys who were able to walk and be away from their mothers were taken to Jerusalem at feast times.

As they grew, children actively participated in the feasts and festivals—events which also helped tie religion to the everyday events of life. Through the various rituals performed at these festivals, the child learned about the history of his nation (Passover), the bountifulness of God toward the people (Feast of Booths), and the righteousness of God (Day of Atonement).

Agriculture was the foremost occupation of Bible people;

thus many of the events emphasized Jewish beliefs about God's acts in nature. The Jews believed that God is in charge of the universe and that many of the natural events which occurred had moral overtones. Rain, sun, and good crops were the reward for righteousness. Difficulties came as a result of sin. No doubt fathers shared many of these beliefs with their sons as they worked the land together. At the time of Passover, the people were instructed to bring the firstfruits of the harvest to the Lord. This was done with great ceremony, and only when the rituals were completed could the new crop be used.

As children observed these rituals, their curiosity was aroused and excellent teaching opportunities were afforded. Parents could explain to their children each year that God controls the universe, that He provides for people, and that He deserves the first and best of all that we have. As Donald Joy has said, children were "immersed in a total curriculum of experience" which included "detailed fundamental teaching/ learning modes as contemporary as Jerome Bruner's 'action, image, and language' forms of representation."[7]

During and after the Exile, the synagogue school played an important part in the religious education of children. We usually think of the synagogue as a place of worship, something like our modern-day church; but actually its main purpose was for instruction. The very name came from the word for "teach." Even the Sabbath services were primarily for teaching rather than for worship.

During the week, the child went to the synagogue to learn to read and study the Law. The basic curriculum, which had to be memorized by the child, included the Shema (doctrinal statement of faith), the Hallel (praise psalms), the story of creation, and the Law (as found in Leviticus). The child also memorized a personal text—a portion of scripture which began with the first letter of his name and ended with the last letter of his name.

Children were taught through a variety of methods, both in the home and in the synagogue school. In the home, visual and other reminders of religion abounded. These were designed to lead naturally to asking questions, which parents were to be prepared to answer. Children actively participated in the religious activities of the family. In the synagogue school, the child was given oral instruction and helped to memorize the

Scriptures. An important part of this memorization process was repeating the words aloud. The Jews felt that unless the child repeated out loud what he had learned, it would soon be forgotten.

The Jewish pattern of religious education was far from perfect; in its worst forms, it bogged down in minutiae and legalism. Nevertheless, the principles on which it was based are as valid today as then. The emphasis on the home, early training of children, repetition, scripture memorization, and a continual relation to life are all elements which need to be emphasized in the religious education of children today. As William Barclay has said, "The Jewish educational ideal has left its mark deeply upon the world because in the last analysis, it aims to educate the child in order to fit him to be a servant of God; it is education of children for God."[8]

The New Testament on Teaching

When we turn to the New Testament, we would expect to find some explicit information about training up children in the Christian way. Knowing Jesus' concern for children, we would also expect to find a record of statements He made concerning conversion and Christian living. On the contrary, He apparently did not enlist children as disciples even in a general sense. The Epistles contain only a few scattered references to the need for fathers to instruct and train their children (Eph. 6:4, for example). One of the Early Church fathers admonished Christians to "train up their children in the knowledge and fear of God."[9]

However, even though references to the religious education of children are few, we again notice *some important principles in practice.* First, children were present in the crowds when Jesus taught, so they often heard what He had to say. They were also involved in the meetings of the early Christians (Acts 21:5). This points out, again, that children were actively involved in the religious life of their parents.

Second, although we do not find Jesus appealing directly to children, He accepted a child's response at whatever level it was given. When children came running to Him, He stopped and took time for them. When they expressed their love to Him in song (Matt. 21:15-16), He expressed appreciation for this.

The boy who gave his lunch to Jesus was certainly not forced; perhaps he was impelled to respond to Jesus because of what he had heard Jesus say that day.

And finally, we still see parents being given specific responsibility for the training of their children. Just as they had taught them the beliefs of Judaism, now Christians were to teach their youngsters the meaning of the Christian life.

One more note about the religious education of the child is given in the New Testament—a rather somber note. In Matt. 18:6 we read this serious warning: "But if anyone causes one of these little ones who believe in me to sin, it would be better for him to have a large millstone hung around his neck and to be drowned in the depths of the sea."

The millstone that Jesus referred to was not the small grinding stone used by women in the house, but rather a large one which required several animals to turn it. To further emphasize the awfulness of causing a child (or young Christian) to sin, Jesus referred to drowning. William Barclay points out that the Jews were afraid of the sea, so the picture of drowning was terrifying to them.

Certainly there is a serious warning here for all who work with children. Jesus knew that children are impressionable. They tend to take words and actions literally and at face value. They are not always able to understand the motives which prompt an action. Therefore, those who are given the task of teaching children must be careful never to do or say anything which could be misinterpreted by the limited understanding of a child.

Implications for Ministry Today

What does all of this say to us about ministry to the children of today? When we compare the conditions under which children live in today's society with those of Bible times, we are struck with a number of major differences. Today most people live in an urban rather than an agricultural society. Christianity does not encompass whole cities, towns, and regions in the way Judaism did. And the home is no longer the stable bulwark that it was then. Are there any principles that we can draw from the examples in the Bible and from ancient Jewish education?

Even though times have changed, there are some very important things that have not. Children are still children, no matter in what era they live. The truths of the Bible remain the same, too. With this in mind, it would seem that the following principles can be applied to Christian education of children today.

1. Christian education needs to begin when the child is young. Today, more than ever before, impressionable young minds need to be filled with the knowledge of God. Children are much more aware of the world around them than were children of years past. If they are old enough to be shaped by the world's false values, they are also old enough to learn about God.

2. We need to capitalize on every opportunity to reach unsaved parents by ministering to children. It is a sad mistake to reach out to children but at the same time to ignore their parents. When we do, the child is set apart from his family, and often tensions are caused with which he cannot cope.

3. The church needs to actively support the home in which the child is being raised. Donald Joy has said:

> When we do, we will provide an environment for children in which we (a) show respect for their value to God, accepting them at their various stages of development and ministering to them in appropriate ways; (b) affirm their childlike faith, and (c) develop a rich display of faithful adherence to the traditions, values, beliefs, and life-styles which are thoroughly and honestly Christian.[10]

This support can come in two forms—ministries to children and ministries to parents. Through a varied program of ministries geared especially to the child, we can support what the Christian parent is doing at home and also reach out to children who do not have a Christian environment. And as we provide help to parents in the education and nurture of their children, we can help to ensure that each child will be surrounded with a Christian influence and that he will be ministered to continually by those who know and love him best.

In all that we do, we must remember that the church school "is at best only an adjunct to the home. It is the parent who is responsible for bringing the child into the world; and it is the parent who is responsible for bringing the child to God. The child is the gift of God to the parent, and the child must be the gift of the parent to God."[11]

4. We need to include children in events when the total Christian community meets together. It is good for children to separate into peer groups for part of their religious education; but it is unwise to do this all the time. A very rich part of a child's religious education is the opportunity to rub shoulders with adult Christians in a variety of settings. The child may not understand all that is said and done, but he cannot help being influenced as he sees Christian adults interacting together, hears them testify to the Lord's goodness, and watches them at prayer and worship.

5. The church needs to be continually concerned about the Christian life of those who teach children. Leaders of children need to be active, growing Christians whose lives can, without shame or doubt, be imitated by children.

Donald Joy has said, "Christian faith is never more than one generation from extinction."[12] If this is so, and I believe it is, then the task of teaching children is an awesome one. We cannot just assume that somehow they will learn about God and adopt His plan for their lives. We must continually and systematically "train a child in the way he should go," praying all the while that "when he is old he will not turn from it" (Prov. 22:6).

REFERENCE NOTES

1. William Barclay, *Train Up a Child: Educational Ideals in the Ancient World* (Philadelphia: Westminster Press, 1959), p. 11.

2. G. Campbell Morgan, *The Gospel According to Matthew* (New York: Fleming H. Revell Co., 1929), p. 97.

3. *Ibid.*

4. William Barclay, *The Gospel of Matthew,* vol. 2 (Philadelphia: Westminster Press, 1958), p. 199.

5. Barclay, *Train Up a Child,* p. 39.

6. Josephus, *Against Apion* 1. 12, cited in Barclay, *Train Up a Child,* p. 12.

7. Donald M. Joy, "Why Teach Children?" in Roy B. Zuck and Robert E. Clark, eds., *Childhood Education in the Church* (Chicago: Moody Press, 1975), p. 12.

8. Barclay, *Train Up a Child,* p. 48.

9. Polycarp, *To the Philippians* 4.2, cited in Barclay, *Train Up a Child,* p. 237.

10. Joy, "Why Teach Children?" p. 20.

11. Barclay, *Train Up a Child,* p. 262.

12. Joy, "Why Teach Children?" p. 18.

*The supreme happiness of life is in
the conviction that we are loved.*
                VICTOR HUGO

3

Meeting the
Needs of Children

In her book *Happily Ever After,* Joy Wilt tells the story of Theresa. Theresa's father died in an accident, leaving her mother a widow. Later, her mother married again; but the new stepfather molested and beat Theresa. One day on her way to school, she was hit by a car, which resulted in a long hospital stay. Because she was out of school for several months, Theresa fell behind in her class and was not able to pass at the end of the year. When she was discharged, she went to a foster home rather than her own.

One day, as Theresa was visiting Joy to work out arrangements for tutoring, an older woman entered the office. As soon as Theresa was out of earshot, the woman exclaimed, "'Ah, to be a child again! No worries, no problems! Life for a child is so simple, so uncomplicated.'"[1]

The film *Cipher in the Snow* tells a similar story. Cliff Evans, a junior high school boy, was on his way to school one day when he asked the bus driver to stop and let him off. As he stepped out of the bus, he dropped dead in the snow. Medical examination later showed that there was nothing physically wrong with him. But plenty of other things had gone wrong in his life. His parents had divorced while he was young, and his new stepfather was a harsh, uncaring man who bullied and criticized Cliff continually. Cliff felt totally unloved at home— a real zero. His feelings about himself soon reflected themselves in his schoolwork, which brought more criticism from his teachers. His schoolmates, thinking he was stupid, left him out of their games and made fun of him. So, at the age of 13, Cliff dropped dead from lack of love.

For most children, childhood is a relatively happy time. They are free of many of the worries that adults must face. But children, like adults, have basic needs. The stories of Theresa and Cliff, though extreme, illustrate what can happen to a child whose basic needs are not met.

Needs determine behavior. If a child's needs are not met satisfactorily, he will try to meet them himself in a variety of ways. As we shall see in the paragraphs to follow, those ways are not always good.

The church—through caring adults—can help to meet many of the child's basic needs for love, security, belonging, significance, and recognition. "In the church's educational program, teachers can express and exhibit God's love to the child. In Christ, the child can find security. In the fellowship of the church, he can find a sense of belonging. In pleasing Jesus and in serving others, he can give love and find self-esteem and recognition."[2]

With this in mind, let us look at some of the basic needs of children.

Children Need Love

Of all the needs of children, the need for love and acceptance is perhaps the most crucial. The love that a child receives forms the basis for his ability to love himself, love others, and love God. Failure to receive love, first from parents, and then from other significant adults in his life, causes many problems for the child. His life becomes a frantic struggle to earn and receive it. And yet, the very fact that he feels he must earn love causes him to feel insecure and unworthy. A child who does not feel loved and accepted also becomes "vulnerable to group pressure. He fights for acceptance from others. He is likely also to feel that God hates him."[3] This child may easily yield to group pressure to experiment with drugs, alcohol, or sex in an attempt to find the acceptance and love he has missed.

A child who receives love feels valued. There are many ways to express love to a child. One way is by sharing our time as well as our possessions, by listening to the child and doing things with him. We also show the child he is loved when we accept him as a unique person and help him to find satisfaction in doing the things he does well. Children need to hear words of love spoken to them. They need to know that parents and teachers enjoy being with them.

Another way to help a child feel loved and valued is to treat him as a person of worth. As you interact with children, use the same courtesies you extend to adults. Let children know that you think highly of them and expect them to do well.

An article in the *Reader's Digest* pointed out that no normal parent (or teacher) gets up in the morning thinking, "How can I make my child feel worthless—unloved—miserable —today?" But that is what happens to children when we do not accept them as they are.

Accepting a child does not mean that we approve of everything he does. It does not mean we allow him to pursue destructive behavior patterns. It does mean that we love him for what he is right now—not for what we would like him to become. This kind of acceptance keeps us from comparing the child negatively with others or criticizing him unduly.

The need for love and acceptance is summed up as follows:

> As a child moves through these years of . . . childhood, his horizons continually widen to encompass experiences and people beyond his home and family. To adjust to new situations that involve possible risks to his self-esteem, he needs to be insulated with feelings of security. He needs to know that while he may reach out for new and exciting adventures, he can depend upon his own world (his family, his church family, his school class) to remain unchanging in its acceptance and support of him.[4]

Children Need a Sense of Personal Worth

Next to love, and very closely related to it, every child needs a sense of self-worth. A sense of self-worth is one of the most important needs of children. A child who feels unloved and worthless will find it hard to adjust to life or to contribute anything to it. As Elizabeth Jones has pointed out, "Living for Christ calls for the highest and best in each of us. It takes determination and courage, and these important qualities need to be developed in childhood."[5]

In the past there has been a great deal of misunderstanding about the feeling of self-worth. Many equated this with pride and warned parents against fostering this pride in their children. Parents were told by one well-known Christian writer never to praise children for fear of causing them to become proud. A whole generation of children grew up under this kind of training, with the result that many adults today feel bad about themselves—inferior and worthless.

Self-esteem is not the same as pride. Rather, it is the deep down understanding that one is a valuable human being, possessing both strengths and weaknesses, loved by God and by others.

A child's sense of personal worth is influenced most of all by the attitudes of his parents toward him. If those adults continually criticize him, compare him with others, laugh at him, or reject him in other ways, his self-esteem will suffer. Unfortunately, the expectations of our society do nothing to help this, says Dr. James Dobson. Beauty and intelligence are two prime values; and children who possess neither suffer in comparison with those who do.

How can parents and teachers help a child develop a sense of personal worth that will support him through the problems and difficulties that go with life? Here are some important ways.

1. Avoid comparing the child with others or making negative comments about him. It is one thing to correct a child's bad behavior, pointing out what he did wrong. It is quite another to constantly tell a child, "You never do anything right," or "You are a liar. I can never trust you." Statements like this reduce a child's feeling of worth and many times cause him to behave in exactly the way you are condemning.

2. Do not ridicule, use sarcasm, or laugh at children. Even laughing at a child's "cute mistakes" can cause him to feel bad about himself. Christopher, age six, noticed that almost every time he opened his mouth, the adults would grin or laugh.

"Why does everyone laugh at me?" he finally asked his mother.

"Oh, they're not laughing at you," replied Mother. "They're laughing with you."

"But I'm not laughing," answered Christopher. Even though the adults in this case meant nothing bad, Christopher felt belittled by their indulgent laughter.

3. Let children help with tasks around the house or at church. When a child learns new skills or performs a task well, he grows in his sense of accomplishment. "Conviction about one's worth comes . . . from feeling that one has important tasks and has met them well" (Bruno Bettelheim). A child who is not allowed to do anything often feels that he is not important and has nothing to contribute to others.

4. Listen to the child when he talks. Talk with him; don't merely throw in an uh-huh every once in a while. When other people are talking to the child, let him do his own answering. When adults answer for children, it gives them the impression that their ideas or opinions do not count.

5. Let children make an increasing number of choices— commensurate with their age and ability. Children have good ideas and can make plans. At the church, let them work together to plan and carry out Bible learning projects and activities. Sometimes you must limit the choices; but whenever possible, give a choice, such as, "Shall we make a mural or diorama?" "Do you want to use chalk, felt markers, or crayons to do your drawing?"

Even children who have had limited opportunities to make choices can be taught to do so. One teacher, working with a group of second graders, helped them to develop their choice-making abilities. The first quarter, she picked the Bible learning project and told the children what they would be doing. Next quarter, she brought to class a list of suggested projects and let pupils choose which one they wished to do. The following quarter, she allowed the children to break into two groups, each group selecting a different project. Finally, near the end of the year, she allowed pupils to work individually or with small groups on a greater number of projects.

6. Help children to experience success more often than failure. This does not mean that a child should never be allowed to fail. We will all meet failure sometime in life and can learn from it. But no child should experience a steady diet of failure. By limiting choices, by helping children set reason-

able goals, and by helping them learn from failure, children grow in their sense of self-worth.

7. Spend time with children. Joy Wilt, in *Happily Ever After,* tells of one occasion when her daughter became quite upset because her mother was leaving to speak at a meeting. Joy promised to bring the child a toy, but that was not what she wanted. She would not be bought off. She wanted her mother's time and attention more than a gift. When we take time to be with children, to talk with them, and to do things with them, we are telling them—even without words—that we think they are important. Children look up to adults. When an adult takes time for a child, this action speaks volumes about the feeling the adult has for the child.

Children Need Security and Discipline

From the day they are born, children experience the need for security. They cry if their needs for food, cuddling, and dry clothing—things which represent security—are not met. Children need to know that they will be cared for, that they are safe, and that they can trust those around them to do what is best for them. The child's sense of security comes from knowing what to expect, and it forms the basis for his ability to trust people and eventually God. A child whose security needs are not met will try to meet those needs for himself. One writer of a book on juvenile delinquency has stated that a child whose security needs are not met will be a thief by the age of eight.[6]

A child experiences physical security when his needs for food, clothing, and shelter are met. But even more important than this is his need for emotional security. If the child enjoys warm, loving relationships, he can often endure lack of security in other areas of life.

Many factors work together to undermine the security of children. Divorce, frequent moves, and lack of discipline are three of the major problems children face. The lack of discipline is especially important. Children who do not receive discipline sense that there are no walls—no protective restrictions in their lives. They become frightened because they do not know where they stand, what is expected of them, or what will happen next.

Sound discipline, on the other hand, lets a child know

that others care about him and about what happens to him. Discipline is not the same thing as just punishment. It involves the "total molding of a child's character through encouraging good behavior and correcting unacceptable behavior."[7] When a child is not disciplined, he fears that he is not loved either. This is illustrated by the story of one girl who—in search of security—stayed out all night. When she returned home the next morning, she hoped her parents would be furious and punish her for her misbehavior. When they did not, she felt they didn't really care about her at all.

A child's sense of security grows when his parents love and care for each other as well as for him, and when his family does things together. It grows when there are regular routines to follow, and regular expectations of him as he participates in homelife. A child grows in security when he is touched lovingly or when he is prayed for by name.

At church, we can help provide children with a sense of security. Here's how.

1. Demonstrate love and affection for each child. One excellent way to do this is to speak to the child as he enters the classroom. Notice new clothes, a missing tooth, a new haircut or hairstyle. Touch children, giving them a pat on the back or a squeeze of the hand. This helps to communicate warmth and bring security. Visits to the child's home also tell him he is loved and valued.

2. Establish regular routines in the classroom and follow them. This does not mean you should adhere to an inflexible schedule; but class format should not change drastically from week to week. This is especially important for young children who find security in the old and familiar.

3. Maintain good discipline. Kindly, but firmly, let children know what behavior limits you expect. Be consistent and fair in enforcing the rules. Also, keep the classroom neat so the child's environment encourages good order. Provide special containers and storage places for supplies, such as scissors and paper, so the children can help you maintain neatness and order.

4. Emphasize God's love for the child. Not all children have the good fortune to grow up in loving homes where parents care about each other and the children. But all children can experience God's love.

I once had a childhood friend who went to church with me and was converted. Her father was an alcoholic and her mother emotionally unstable. Gladys' only security in life came from her relationship with God. She was saved, both emotionally and spiritually, through that relationship.

Children Need Praise

Recently, the American Institute of Family Relations asked a group of mothers to record the number of times they made negative and positive statements to their children. The results were thought-provoking. Mothers reported that they criticized 10 times more than they gave favorable comments.

The seriousness of this fact is readily seen when one considers that seldom do we change a behavior by criticizing it. Change is much more easily and permanently effected through praise. And, concluded the test, it takes four positive statements to counteract the effects of one negative one.[8]

Psychologists and educators have discovered that when we praise a child, we encourage him to live up to our estimate of his potential. Conversely, when we criticize, we also set a standard for him to live up to—but it is a negative standard. Furthermore, criticism lowers a child's self-esteem, making it harder than ever for him to perform well. Liberal amounts of honest praise can have a beneficial effect on even a very discouraged child.

When praising children, keep these guidelines in mind.

1. Praise the child for what he does, not for what he is. Sometimes a child will behave well even when he is feeling mean or naughty inside. A statement like, "You were a good boy this morning," makes him feel even guiltier—and may cause him to break out into bad behavior. Instead say, "I appreciate the way you colored quietly this morning." This type of praise honestly recognizes what the child did—no matter what his feelings were at the time.

2. Praise a child for his accomplishments, not his innate abilities or looks. A child has no control over his personal beauty or intelligence. To praise a child for these things is to praise him for something he had nothing to do with. But we can praise a child for what he has done with what he was given.

For example, "I know you tried your best. Keep up the good work." Or, "You did a good job making your bed today."

3. Be sincere. Children can readily spot phony praise.

4. Praise the child as soon as possible after he has done something well.

5. Praise the child for his effort, even if he fails. We cannot always succeed; but an honest effort should always be praised. It is very comforting to a child who has failed to know that you know he did his very best—and can improve in the future.

Children Need Opportunities to Take Responsibility, Make Choices, and Be Creative

At first glance, these three needs may appear to be very different from one another. But they are quite closely related— and very important to a child's healthy growth and development.

The need to learn to make choices cannot be overestimated, especially when we relate this to a child's spiritual development. The whole of the Christian experience involves the ability to make choices. The person must first make the choice to receive Jesus as Savior and to give his entire life to Him. Following that major choice, he must make hundreds of smaller daily choices as he lives out his Christian commitment.

The ability to make a choice involves several factors. The person must understand what choice-making really is—selecting one thing and rejecting others. He must be able to weigh the consequences of his choice, and then stick with his decision even when it is not easy or pleasant.

Children who are not allowed to make choices as they grow up experience difficulty in the Christian life. They find it difficult to make a decision for Christ and to stick by it.

How can children learn to make choices? One way is by giving them responsibilities which they must carry out. When a child has tasks to perform, he has opportunities to decide when they will be done and how. He learns to live with the consequences of choices—whether they be good or bad. He also learns the rewards of choosing well and following through.

Creative activity also offers children opportunities for making choices. The child can select materials he wants to use and combine them in a way which reflects his unique personality, thoughts, and abilities. As children work out their ideas in creative activity, they reap the rewards of accomplishment. They also sense that God has created them special, and they discover gifts they can use in His service.

At church, we can help to fulfill these needs of children. Beginning with the very young, we can train children to take responsibility—for putting away books and toys, for caring for the church property, and for being kind and good to those around them. Through creative Bible learning activities we can provide children with numerous opportunities to express their personalities in creative work. And, as we teach them about Jesus, we can offer them chances to choose Him as Savior and Lord.

Children Need God

Dorie, the true story of missionary Doris Van Stone, is one of the most moving accounts I have ever read. For some inexplicable reason the mother loved Dorie's little sister but totally rejected Dorie. On one occasion, her mother said, "Judge, I'd have gotten rid of her before she was born if I could have."[9] While Dorie was still a young child, she and her sister were placed in an orphanage, where Dorie was regularly beaten and mistreated. Foster homes, later on, proved no different. In some she was mistreated; in others the attitude was one of total indifference. Finally, as a young adult, Dorie was able to establish contact with her father. But eventually he also rejected her totally.

By anyone's reckoning, Dorie should have grown up to be a social misfit or worse. But when she was 12 years old, something happened which changed the entire course of her life.

At a children's meeting one day, Dorie heard the message, "God loves you." At first she rejected the idea. Nobody loves me! she thought. But somehow, when the worker repeated the statement again, God worked in the heart of this 12-year-old girl. She believed the truth and found peace and joy. The circumstances of her life did not improve for many years; but because she had experienced God's love for herself, Dorie's life was changed. When she was grown, she became one of the first missionaries to penetrate the jungles of New Guinea and take the gospel there.

Certainly not many adults can point to a childhood conversion as dramatic as this one; but the fact remains that young children need the love and security they can find only in God. Even as children, they have spiritual needs which can be met as they learn to know about God, have a personal relationship with Him, and try to please Him.

Even though the Bible is a book written for adults, not children, there are many important truths about God which children can understand and appropriate to their lives. Belief in God can also give them the proper foundation for right values in today's changing world.

How can children learn to know and love God? Many of their concepts about Him will come as they experience God's love reflected by the important adults in their lives (parents and teachers). As illustrated by the experience of Dorie, it is not impossible for a child to sense God's love even when he does not experience love from anyone else. But how much more difficult it becomes. God's love takes on so much more meaning when the child receives love from others. And as he grows up seeing adults living sincerely for God, he finds models he can safely imitate.

These then are some of the basic needs of children—needs that we can help to meet through our ministry to them. In the following chapters of this book, we will explore ways and means of ministering to children at the church and through the church.

REFERENCE NOTES

1. Joy Wilt, *Happily Ever After* (Waco, Tex.: Word Books, 1977), p. 147.

2. Mary L. Hammach, "Personality Development of Children," in Roy B. Zuck and Robert E. Clark, eds., *Childhood Education in the Church* (Chicago: Moody Press, 1975), p. 46.

3. John Drescher, *Seven Things Children Need* (Scottdale, Pa.: Herald Press, 1976), p. 58.

4. Barbara Bolton and Charles T. Smith, *Creative Bible Learning* (Glendale, Calif.: Regal Books, 1977), p. 32.

5. Elizabeth Jones, *Teaching Primaries Today* (Kansas City: Beacon Hill Press of Kansas City, 1974), p. 36.

6. Drescher, *Seven Things Children Need,* pp. 35-36.

7. *Ibid.,* p. 109.

8. *Ibid.,* p. 99.

9. Doris Van Stone with Erwin Lutzer, *Dorie: The Girl Nobody Loved* (Chicago: Moody Press, 1979), p. 48.

To the Jewish Rabbis, it was as great a
privilege to teach a child the Law, as it
was to have received it on Mount Sinai
from the hands of God.
                    WILLIAM BARCLAY

Ministering to
Preschool Children

During the first five years of life, the child learns more than
he will at any other period of his life. The question is not,
"Will he learn?" but rather, "What will he learn?" and "How
best can we help him to learn?"

In order to best provide for the spiritual training of preschoolers at church, we need to understand their needs and
characteristics. When we know what nursery and kindergarten
children are like, we are then able to plan rooms, provide
equipment and supplies, and design learning activities which
will promote maximum spiritual growth.

In this chapter, we will look first at the characteristics
of preschoolers, birth through five years. We will then consider
the space and equipment requirements for nursery children and
for kindergarten children. Following this, we will discuss learning activities appropriate to both nursery and kindergarten preschoolers.

CHARACTERISTICS

Characteristics of Children—0-15 Months

During the first 12-15 months of life, the child grows from
a helpless infant (6-9 pounds, 18-22 inches) to an active toddler

(17-24 pounds, 28-31 inches) who can sit, stand, walk, and perform a number of other physical skills. During this same period, the child also experiences rapid development mentally, emotionally, and socially.

To minister to the baby, it is vitally important to meet his physical needs in an atmosphere of love. All of his development in other areas hinges on the way his physical needs are met. When these are adequately provided for, the child grows in trust and security which form the foundation for his entire life. If from his earliest experiences in church the child has the awareness of loving care, he will find it easier to realize and trust the loving care of the Lord Jesus.

Characteristics of Children—12-24 Months

PHYSICAL

Has learned to walk, but may be unsteady on feet. By two can climb up and down steps. May be able to walk backward.

Weighs 33-36 pounds; is 32-34 inches tall.

Usually is not toilet trained.

Large muscles developing; full of energy, but tires easily. Likes push-pull toys which utilize large muscles.

Fine muscles developed enough to feed self and manipulate some toys. Can grasp with finger and thumb.

Learns to build small block tower (four blocks), pull off cap and socks, and unscrew lids.

Assimilates environment through taste and touch.

MENTAL

Can say, "Mama," "Dada," and two or three other words.

Single word often stands for whole sentence.

By two can understand 250-300 words; can combine words to express thought in simple sentence.

Language is mostly nouns and verbs.

Can name objects in a book.

Points to body parts when named.

Has brief attention span, short memory.

Loves repetition of favorite stories.

Needs positive directions rather than negative.

SOCIAL

Concerned only about self; wants to do things for self.

Views other children as inanimate objects. Pokes and pushes them in same way he does other objects.

Likes to be near other children, but does not play with them; age of "parallel play."

Older toddlers may imitate household activities; may help with simple tasks.

Can indicate wants without crying.

EMOTIONAL

Shows wide range of emotions: affection, delight, fear, disgust.

Fears being separated from parents; finds security in familiar people, procedures, and surroundings.

Impulsive; goes overboard with new experiences.

Often acts out feelings in play.

SPIRITUAL

Is open and receptive.

Believes what he is told.

Needs simple Bible truths repeated often.

Can experience happy feelings associated with God.

Characteristics of Children—2-3 Years

PHYSICAL

Weighs 35-40 lbs.
Is small, but not a miniature adult.
Is active, but tires easily.
Needs up to 12 hours sleep at night, plus a rest during the day.
Large muscles developing; small muscles not well developed.
Cannot use crayons or scissors with skill.
Learning to dress self. Can manage all but tying shoes and buttoning back buttons by about age three.
Cannot do two things at once (sing and finger play).
Vocal cords not well developed; should not be urged to sing loudly.
Is susceptible to disease.
Learns through the senses.
Has short attention span.

MENTAL

Has limited vocabulary of 300-900 words.
Has short attention span—2 to 4½ minutes.
"Reads" pictures.
Loves stories about self.
Learns through imitation and by asking questions.
Learns through senses.
By three can begin to draw distinguishable pictures.
Can make simple things from clay or sand.
Can sing in group.
Cannot understand symbolism, time, space, or distance.
Cannot distinguish between fact and fantasy.
Memory undependable; cannot easily remember from week to week.
Learns through repetition of favorite stories and songs.

SOCIAL

A loner. Often plays alone even in a group. Just learning to play with others.
Possessive of toys. May hit or grab to get or protect toys.
Self-centered; world revolves around self. Should not be confused with selfishness.
May have imaginary playmates.
May be timid. Clings to mother and familiar things.
Dependent on others to help him. Just learning to do things for self.
Can learn to "help" if given supervision.
Wants to please.
Wants attention.
Can share ideas with others.

EMOTIONAL

Has sensitive nervous system. Easily upset by noise and confusion.
Cries easily.
Has many fears. May have bad dreams.
Needs the security of old familiar routines, places, and people.
Says no often, even when he really means something else.
May have temper tantrums as a way of getting what he wants.
Actions often based on feelings.
Power of choice not developed enough to show him what is best.

SPIRITUAL

Trusting; believes what teachers and parents tell him.
Is easily pliable.
Has a "hunger" for God; asks questions about God.
Can learn simple Bible truths and songs, such as: "God loves you," or "God made the world."
Cannot understand religious symbolism.
Can express love to God and talk with Him.
"Catches" religion from the example of those around him.

Characteristics of Children—4-5 Years

PHYSICAL

Period of rapid growth. Fives losing chubby baby look.

Child is proud of his growth. Wants to be "big" but in reality is still quite little.

Large muscles developing rapidly. Needs exercise. Child experiences real pain if forced to sit still for too long.

Restless, always on the move. Runs, jumps, moves quickly. Fatigues easily.

Needs alternating periods of rest and activity to avoid overfatigue.

Small muscles developing, but not dependable. Child may not be able to color in lines, cut straight, or manage buttons and bows on clothing.

Needs large crayons and paintbrushes, blunt scissors, and large work and play areas.

Some fives learning to print.

Is susceptible to disease.

Eyes and ears easily strained.

MENTAL

Curious; wants to know. May take things apart to find out how they work.

Understands 1,500-2,300 words, but uses only about a third of them.

Loves to talk. Able to put thoughts and ideas into words. Loves to ask questions.

Loves to experiment with words, but may not always really understand the words he uses. Loves sounds of words.

Cannot always differentiate between fact and fantasy.

Suggestible. Acts on slightest suggestion. Believes what adults tell him.

Limited understanding of time, space, and distance. May say "yesterday" to tell about something that happened a week ago.

Forgets easily.

Literal minded. Does not understand symbolism.

Learns best through his senses, through play, and by imitating those around him.

Can memorize, but does not always understand meaning of what he has learned. Memory activity should emphasize understanding rather than just rote repetition.

Enjoys pictures, records, and books.

SOCIAL

Beginning to play in small groups with other children. Feels left out if not accepted by them.

Tends to be a conformist, especially at age five.

Beginning to respect property rights of others, but needs help in learning to share and take turns.

Basically self-centered. Talks about self a lot. May brag about self.

Identifies with adults; wants their attention and approval.

Wants to be a helper, to gain approval.

Likes to show adults what he can (or did) do.

May be unwilling to share the attention of an adult with other children.

Testing his world. May misbehave to see how far he will be allowed to go, but wants and needs limits.

EMOTIONAL

Emotions intense and close to surface. Laughs, cries, and loves easily.

May explode into anger, but outbursts are generally short-lived.

Fear is a predominant emotion.

Child often reflects the emotions of adults around him.

May be shy or jealous.

Sense of humor beginning to develop.

Beginning to understand and empathize with the feelings of others.

SPIRITUAL

Thinks of God in a personal way. Often thinks of Him as a giant, "larger than life" person with supernatural powers.

Sometimes confuses God and Jesus.

Trusts God and other people. Thinks of Jesus as a loving friend.

Able to pray and worship.

Beginning to recognize right and wrong, but may blame others for his wrongdoing.

Spiritual concepts closely related to the people he knows. Spiritual growth closely tied to emotional maturity.

ROOMS, EQUIPMENT, AND MATERIALS

Rooms for Nursery Children

Rooms for babies, toddlers, twos, and threes should be as clean, cheerful, and attractive as the church can make them. Nursery children are bundles of energy and perpetual motion; therefore, the first requirement for a nursery room is space. Try to provide at least 25 square feet per child; 35 square feet is better. If possible, place babies, toddlers, twos, and threes in separate rooms with no more than 12 babies, toddlers, or twos per room, and no more than 15 threes.

Nursery rooms should be located on the first floor of the church, near—but not too near—parents' classes. Avoid placing the rooms near the sanctuary. Glass windows into the auditorium and loudspeakers in the nursery cause confusion and disturb the children.

Following is a sketch of a suggested floor plan for the Nursery Department.

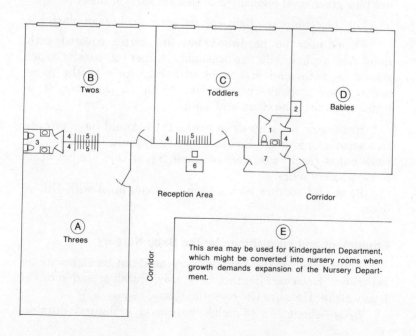

1. Adult washroom—shared by workers in Rooms C and D
2. Babies' change table—cabinet for supplies above
3. Children's toilet facilities (child-sized fixtures—two commodes, two lavatories)—shared by Rooms A and B
4. Coatracks—teachers
5. Coatracks—children (supply cabinet above)
6. Secretary's desk
7. Service area—accessible to all groups—may be equipped with bottle warmers, small refrigerator, and cabinets for storage of food and supplies for extended sessions.

Rectangular rooms work best for arranging learning centers. A good proportion is three-fourths as wide as long. The rooms should be well lighted and well ventilated, with clear glass windows that are low enough for children to see out when they are standing on the floor.

Drapes should be washable and quite plain.

Walls and *woodwork* should be painted in soft, solid colors. Pale yellow or a rich ivory are good for a northern exposure; use blue green on the southern or western sides of the church.

For the *ceiling,* use light-colored acoustical tile or plaster.

Floors may be hardwood but are better covered with linoleum, asphalt tile, or washable carpet or rugs. Carpet should be plain and in a color to harmonize with the room decor. Since nursery children like to sit on the floor, it is important that it be clean and warm.

Heaters or *registers* close to the floor should have protective screens or shields. Electrical outlets should be located on walls out of reach of nursery children. Those that are not need to have safety plugs.

Baby and toddler rooms should be equipped with Dutch doors.

Equipment and Furnishings for the Baby Nursery

Equipment for the baby nursery need not be elaborate or expensive. However, it must be sturdy, durable, and scrupulously clean. Here are the essential items.

Beds—about 27 x 48 inches, hardwood, in natural, durable

finish. If desired, provide a few small beds, 18 x 36, for babies under six months. Since adequate air circulation is important, avoid built-in beds. Place beds two to three feet apart. Babies who attend regularly should have the same bed each week. This way, the child's feeding schedule and other instructions can be attached to the bed.

A bottle warmer. If toddlers must share the room with the babies, keep this out of their reach.

Smock-type uniforms in pastel colors for workers. Use the same color for all workers in one room.

Storage cabinet built high on the wall. Use this for linens, supplies, uniforms, and toys.

A moderate-size *wooden rocking chair* without upholstery

A Bible. Even babies will notice the worker using this.

A few safe, durable, plastic, rubber, or wooden *toys.* These should be finished with nontoxic paint.

Books, pictures, crib toys, and mobiles

If finances permit, the following items are also nice: a record player, nursery records, a baby jumper, and a playpen.

It is essential to keep the baby nursery as clean and healthful as possible. Not only does this help to prevent sickness in babies, but it encourages parents to leave their children in the nursery instead of taking them to class or worship service. Be sure to:

- Wash walls, woodwork, and floors as necessary.
- Insist that workers wash hands frequently.
- Launder all linens each week.
- Wash toys and other equipment frequently with soap and water or a cleaning solution.
- Have a first-aid kit available.
- Isolate children with colds or other symptoms of illness.

Equipment and Furnishings for Toddlers, Twos, and Threes

The amount of furniture and equipment for toddlers, twos, and threes will depend on the size of the class and the space available. The diagram which follows shows a room for toddlers, twos, or threes with suitable furnishings arranged to allow adequate space for learning activities.

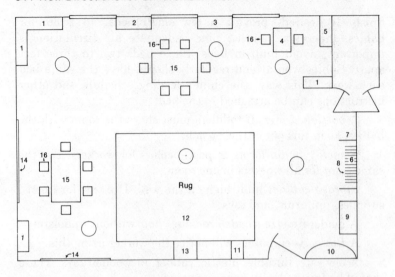

1. Open shelves with closed back (30" to 36" wide, 27" high, 11" deep)
2. Bookrack with slanting shelves (35" wide, 30" high, 12" to 14" deep at base)
3. Puzzle rack (26" high shelves with sliding doors for storage)
4. Tea table (18" wide, 24" long, top 18" from floor)
5. Doll bed (16" wide, 28" long; sturdy enough to hold a child)
6. Coatrack for children
7. Coatrack for teachers
8. High storage cabinet for supplies (built over children's coatrack)
9. Teachers' desk and picture file
10. Rocking boat (reversed, it is a set of steps; when not in use, it can be stored on side against wall)
11. Record player (on table 16" high, top 12" wide, 18" long)
12. Rug (at least 9' x 12'—unnecessary if room is carpeted)
13. Bible table (18" x 24" and 18" high; can be as small as 12" x 18" if space is limited)
14. Tack boards or bulletin boards (24" high, 6' to 8' long; lower edge 24" to 26" from floor); felt covered or cork
15. Table 30" wide, 48" long, top 20" from floor
16. Chairs (seat 10" from floor; one for each child unnecessary)

Materials and Supplies for Toddlers, Twos, and Threes

Toddlers and two- and three-year-olds learn through their senses and by doing. Therefore, the nursery rooms for these children should contain materials which the children can see, touch, hear, smell, and handle. The following items are recommended. Items with a ● should especially be included in a toddler room. Later in the chapter, we will consider ways to use these materials effectively in activity learning centers.

☐ Autoharp or ChromAharP is a desirable substitute for piano
☐ Ball—8" or 9" in diameter
☐ Bible—a sturdy, large-print, stiff-back Bible
☐ Blockbuster blocks—large, hollow, reinforced cardboard
☐ Blocks, wooden—standard nursery educational units
☐ Block accessories:
   Wooden car or truck—18" long
   Interlocking wooden train
   Stand-up figures, wooden or unbreakable plastic—people and animals
☐ Books—as recommended in *Toddler Teacher* and *Nursery Teacher*
☐ Construction paper—assorted colors
☐ Crayons (7/16")—jumbo
☐ Dishes, soft plastic
☐ Doll bed equipment—mattress, sheets, blanket
☐ Doll clothes—sturdy, washable
☐ Dolls—two or three—unbreakable, soft plastic or vinyl, with molded hair
☐ Drawing paper or newsprint—12" x 18"
☐ Felt or flannel—for covering bulletin boards and making figures
☐ Full-length mirror
☐ Modeling clay—Play-Doh or a homemade dough in assorted colors
☐ ● Push-pull toys
☐ Puzzles, wooden—as recommended in *Toddler Teacher* and *Nursery Teacher*
☐ Puzzle rack, wire—holds 12 puzzles
☐ Record player
☐ Rest mats—plastic covered foam pads, small cotton rugs, or large Turkish towels; for extended session
☐ Rhythm instruments

☐ Rocking boat
☐ Scissors—a few small, blunt pairs for nursery children
☐ Seals—as recommended in *Toddler Teacher* and *Nursery Teacher*
☐ Soft, cuddly animals
☐ ● Supplies—extra diapers, training panties, soap, washcloths, powder, safety pins, information cards (from *Toddler Bible Take Homes,* Set 1), pencils, bottle warmer, plastic bags for wet diapers, paper trash bags (to be taped high on wall)
☐ Telephones—two, plastic
☐ Wrapping paper (brown), newsprint, or shelf paper for long posters and friezes[1]

Rooms for Kindergarten Children

When planning the rooms for kindergartners, follow the same principles for choosing drapes, paint, ceiling and floor coverings, and safety features for heaters and electrical outlets. Like nursery children, kindergartners also need space in which to move about—at least 25-30 square feet per child. Try to choose a room which has windows equal to one-fifth or one-fourth of its wall space, and which is near an outside entrance.

Equipment and Furnishings for Kindergarten Children

Provide as many of the following items as you have finances to purchase and space to store. The diagram of a nursery department (on page 51) shows one way to arrange the room. Ideas are given later in this chapter for ways to adapt to a "too small" room.

1. Coatracks for pupils (34"-36" from the floor, 5'-6' long). Provide a shelf on top for storing caps and other personal belongings.
2. Coatracks for workers
3. Wall supply cabinets for teachers' materials
4. Low, open shelves, for storing materials the children use and help to put away. (Shelves should be 36"-40" wide, 36"-42" high, 12"-16" deep, with 12"-14" space between. Shelves this size are large enough to store larger items like a record player.)

5. Bulletin boards (27"-29" from the floor; 3' x 4'). Have these on one or two walls, made from Celutex, cork, or pegboard. Add a tray along the bottom to use as a picture rail.
6. Tables, rectangular (20"-22" high, 10" higher than the chair seats). A table 30" wide allows children to sit on both sides and gives room in the middle for supplies (30" x 48" or 60" is a good size).
7. Bible table (24" x 36", 18" x 22" high)
8. Other small tables 20" x 30", 22"-24" high). Use for the wonder table and other interest centers.
9. Chairs—sturdy, but light enough for the children to carry. Seats should be 10"-12" from the floor. Use 10" chairs for fours and 12" chairs for fives. If you have fours and fives combined, provide 10" chairs for all. You also need a junior-size chair for the lead teacher and one or two adult-size chairs for visitors.
10. Bookrack (36" wide with two or three shelves)
11. Painting easels. Use double easels with attached trays for holding paint. Trays should be 18"-23" from the floor.
12. Piano—studio size (optional)

Materials and Supplies for Kindergarten Rooms

- ☐ Autoharp or ChromAharP (substitute for piano)
- ☐ Bible
- ☐ Blocks—standard wooden building; block accessories described in the *Kindergarten Teacher*
- ☐ Books—as recommended in *Kindergarten Teacher*
- ☐ Brushes—¾" long-handled
- ☐ Construction paper—assorted colors
- ☐ Crayons
- ☐ Dishes—soft plastic—and other home-living supplies recommended in *Kindergarten Teacher*
- ☐ Doll bed and furnishings—mattress, sheets, blanket
- ☐ Dolls and clothes
- ☐ Dress-up clothes
- ☐ Figures—stand-ups of people and animals
- ☐ Filmstrips—as recommended in *Kindergarten Teacher*
- ☐ First-aid kit
- ☐ Manila paper—12" x 18"
- ☐ Masking tape

☐ Nature materials—plants, aquarium
☐ Newsprint—12" x 18" and 18" x 24"
☐ Paints—finger and poster
☐ Pictures and other resources provided in *Kindergarten Teaching Resources, Kindergarten Activities, Kindergarten Bible Stories,* and *Listen*
☐ Picture file
☐ Puzzles and puzzle rack
☐ Record player—three speeds, manually operated
☐ Rocker—child size

General Guidelines for Furnishing Preschool Rooms

When selecting furnishings, equipment, and materials for preschoolers, keep these guidelines in mind.

1. Be sure they are durable and lasting. For toddlers, twos, and threes the doll bed should be large enough for a child to climb into. Blocks, cars, and other toys should be strong enough to withstand children who sit, stand, or walk on them. Avoid small plastic or metal cars, dishes, and miscellaneous toys. Not only do these get lost easily and tend to create clutter, but they are quite breakable. They may encourage children to be destructive.

2. All toys should be safe. Bright, attractive paint is not enough; be sure the paint is nontoxic and that there are no sharp corners or other hazardous features.

3. Equipment should be economical. This is not the same as cheap. Often a more expensive item is really more economical because it will last longer. If your budget is limited, enlist parents or teachers to make some toys or pieces of equipment.

4. Materials should allow the child to learn through his senses, through exploration, and by doing. Toys need not be expensive or highly mechanized to satisfy this criterion. Clay, for example, is one of the best tools to use with preschool children. It is inexpensive and simple; yet it allows them to learn through the sense of touch, and to be creative. When purchasing items for the nursery and kindergarten classes, look for items that the children can use in many different ways.

When Space and Materials Are Limited

Very few churches are able to provide an "ideal" classroom

for nursery children. However, all churches can provide good rooms. Even when rooms are small, or less than perfect in other ways, they can be made attractive and useful.

1. If overcrowding is the problem, take a look at what is in the room. Space is more important than furniture. Remove unnecessary tables and chairs—and all clutter.

2. Try to provide the most adequate room possible for the nursery class, twos and threes. In some churches, thoughtful adults have volunteered to take less suitable rooms so the nursery class could have better facilities.

3. Use portable equipment. If there is no room available for nursery twos and threes, use a portion of the church sanctuary. Put equipment, such as storage cabinets, on wheels so they can be removed at the end of class. Use items like bookshelves to form partitions for the class.

ENVIRONMENT AND METHODS

A Good Learning Environment for Preschool Children

When we speak of the proper learning environment for nursery and kindergarten children, we are talking about more than the sum total of the materials available to them. Rooms, space, location, furnishings, and equipment are all important. But more important is the spirit or atmosphere of the Preschool Department. The appearance of the room, the child's interaction with other children and adults, the pictures he sees, and the things he hears and does—all form the environment for the child. Here the teacher is the key. Ample space and expensive equipment may be of little value unless preschoolers are immersed in an atmosphere of warmth created by a wise, loving, and Christlike teacher.

To ensure a good learning environment for preschool children, these things are essential.

● Workers need to be warm, loving, and Christlike. They must understand the preschool child and have a desire to work with him. A worker who has this desire will spend the class time interacting with the children, not indulging in friendly chitchat with other workers. He or she will do everything possible to make sure that the child has a happy and productive experience at church.

● Rooms need to be clean, neat, and orderly, even if they cannot be perfect in other ways. At the end of each session, workers should help the children put away toys, books, dolls, and other equipment. Not only does this help to provide an orderly room for the children, but it teaches them to be cooperative and helpful.

● Equipment should be relevant to the unit being studied —and in good condition. Materials not in active use should be stored. Broken materials should be removed. Even the contents of cabinets and storage areas should be kept neat and in good order. Care for all these details results in a calm, orderly atmosphere for the child.

● Never forget that rooms teach. Each teacher must make the best possible use of room and facilities to provide a good learning environment for the spiritual development of young children.

Ways the Preschool Child Learns

Preschoolers learn through their senses, especially the sense of touch. Watch any young child. In order to "see" something, he has to touch and handle it. He is not content just to look at an object; he wants to pick it up, pinch it, poke it, and fondle it. Young preschoolers go a step further and put everything into their mouths. Without these experiences, they cannot really understand what things are like.

Not only do preschoolers learn as they touch, but also when they see, taste, smell, and hear. Therefore, teachers of preschoolers need to provide a variety of materials and activities which appeal to and involve the child's five senses. Preschool rooms should contain pretty pictures, manipulative toys, nature items, and musical instruments.

Preschoolers also learn through play activity. To a young child, play is as important as work is to an adult. In fact, for the child, play is work. Through play, the child reproduces actions he has seen. He experiments with materials and finds new ways to use them. He develops emotional and physical control and learns how to interact socially with others.

To meet the child's needs, guided play activities should be a vital part of any learning experience for preschoolers. The key word is *guided.* At church, we do not turn children loose in a roomful of toys and require only that they enjoy themselves. Instead, we guide their play to help them learn important spiritual concepts. Notice these different ways a teacher can guide a preschooler as he plays.

A child is ready to use the blocks: "Jimmy, would you like to build a church? Church is God's house. We like the church."

Two children both want to be the mommy at the home-living center: "Anne, you may be the mother. Teresa, this family needs a grandmother, too. Could you be Grandmother and rock the baby?"

A group of children is making a mural: "James, I like the pretty sun you drew. God made the sun. Thank You, God, for the sun."

Not all play is guided in the sense that it is teacher-directed. Sometimes the guidance comes through the kinds of materials provided.

Another way children learn is when their curiosity is aroused, causing them to ask questions. Children do not sit still and listen when adults talk; but when we provide a rich environment, with many things which cause them to ask "Why?" "What?" or "How?" we can then teach the child as we talk informally. As we answer a preschooler's questions, he learns many things.

Preschoolers learn when they engage in a variety of experiences. A child learns to paint when he is allowed to paint. He learns about life when he accompanies parents to the store, to church, and to other places. Children need varied experiences at church too. Instead of just showing them pictures of flowers, take them on a walk to see and smell the flowers. Let them visit the pastor's study or watch the janitor at work. Guide them to work together to make a picture book for a sick friend. As children participate in such experiences, they learn about God, the church, and Christian living in a way they never would by hearing us tell them, "God is good," or "Be ye kind."

Imitation and imagination are two other factors which contribute to a preschooler's learning. Even young children watch those about them and see what they do. Later, the child tries to imitate those actions—putting himself in the place of another person. As the child does this, he grows in his understanding of people and of the world. This imaginative, imitation play also helps the child to develop attitudes and habits.

These principles describing how preschoolers learn help us to know what sorts of activities we should provide for them at church.

Teaching the Preschool Child

As we look at the needs and characteristics of preschool children, it becomes readily apparent how we *cannot* teach them. We do not make them sit still and listen. We do not ask them to work in a group, to color in lines, or stay with an activity for a long period of time. Instead, we provide a variety of informal activities which capture their attention—though only briefly—and involve them totally in the learning experience. Most of these activities need to be arranged at learning (activity or interest) centers to which the child comes and works informally. Older preschoolers—(age 2½ and above) will also profit from a brief large-group time. The length of this varies with the age of the child. Young children may stay with the group for only a few minutes before wandering off. Kindergarten children will usually remain interested for 5 to 10 minutes. Follow the guidance given in the *Toddler, Nursery,* and *Kinder-. garten* teaching manuals for planning informal and large-group activities.

As the children come to interest centers, the teacher may interact with them individually or in small groups of two or three. Using guided conversation to direct the child's activity, he can teach him spiritual truths related to the activity he is pursuing.

Here are activities especially suited to the needs and interests of preschoolers.

Blocks. Blocks are one of the most important learning tools in preschool classrooms. As the child uses blocks, he has an opportunity for large-muscle activity. He can work alone or in cooperation with one or two other children. He has a chance to think and create. And he can also learn important spiritual truths.

Younger preschoolers often just hold blocks or carry them around. Threes begin to try building block towers—stacking two, three, or four blocks one on top of the other. Kindergartners are able to build objects, many of which look quite realistic.

Pictures posted in the block corner suggest to the child some things he may build. Through guided conversation, the teacher can suggest other objects which relate to the unit of study. For example, in a unit on the church, children can build block churches. When community helpers is the emphasis, the possibilities for block creations are almost endless.

For older children, block accessories are helpful. Provide figures of people, and small cars and trucks. The child can use these to play out various roles or situations after he has finished building.

Even two-year-olds can begin to learn to help put away the blocks, thus learning an important lesson in Christian living. Threes, fours, and fives should be encouraged to share blocks and work together.

Home-Living Center. To the preschool child, home is the center of his existence. It is natural, then, for him to imitate through play in the home-living center what he sees and hears at home. As he does, he has an opportunity to take the roles of the adults he has observed. At first, the child will imitate his mother, father, and other members of the family, because these are the people with whom he has had the most experience. As his world broadens, he may also take the parts of community helpers (storekeepers, mailmen) and people he sees at church.

Play in the home-living center helps a child to act out his feelings of joy, concern, fear, or anger. When adults have these feelings, they often talk them over with a friend. A preschooler's verbal ability is limited, but playing out the feelings has the same beneficial effect for him that talking does for an adult.

In the home-living center pupils also have opportunities to put into practice such Christian principles as kindness, sharing, helping, caring for others, and taking turns. This will require the guidance of the teacher; but as the child grows older, it is helpful to let him live out these experiences for himself as much as possible.

Play in the home-living center also helps the child to grow in self-esteem. At home, there are many things he is not allowed to do. He cannot touch the stove, adjust the TV, or pick up the baby. These are wise and necessary restrictions, but they may make the child feel small and inadequate. In the home-experience, express a feeling, or give direction. Children always living center, he can try out these adult activities and grow in his feelings of competence.

Young children play alone, doing solitary activities such as rocking a doll or "cooking" a meal. Older children become more involved and more verbal in their play. They will act out whole homelife sequences, such as caring for a baby, fixing a meal and eating it, or entertaining guests. They also like lots of props—furniture, dress-up clothes, and varied accessories. Be sure to provide homelife items for boys as well as girls.

A wise teacher can easily guide play in the home-living center to relate to Christian concepts. Sometimes this guidance will relate to the children's behavior through the suggestion of kind and loving actions. At other times, specific activities will be suggested, such as "Don, would you like to thank God for the food today?" The materials the teacher puts in the home-living center will also spark ideas for unit-related play. In a unit on God's gifts of food, provide empty food boxes and cans so children can "cook" pudding, vegetables, and other foods. Then talk about God's care in providing these good things to eat.

Puzzles, Beads, and Pegboards. These materials are especially good in helping the preschooler develop the ability to do and to achieve. When a child learns to put a puzzle together, or forms an interesting design with beads or pegs, he feels the thrill of accomplishment—"I did it!" The child learns to think and reason, to solve problems, and to create. He also learns the wise use of materials as the teacher instructs him in the correct way to use the puzzle or beads.

Wooden inlay puzzles are the best investment for preschool children. They will last for years and are easier for the young child to manipulate than thin cardboard puzzles. For younger preschoolers, provide puzzles in which each piece is a complete object—dog, cat, fruit, or person. Older children can work increasingly difficult puzzles with up to 20 or more pieces. There will, of course, be vast differences in the individual abilities of pupils to work puzzles.

Even puzzles which are not especially "religious" in theme can be used to teach Christian truths. For example, when a child works a puzzle showing a boy on a tricycle, the teacher can say, "Jerry is big enough to ride a tricycle. God helps Jerry to grow bigger and stronger. Thank You, God." A teacher can also relate to the child's ability to work the puzzle (or use beads or pegs creatively) to spiritual truth. For example, "I like the way you put pretty pegs on your board, Tammy. God gave you eyes to see pretty colors. Thank You, God, for eyes."

Books and Stories. From their earliest years, children need to have and enjoy books. Not only do books bring pleasure to the child, but they also offer opportunities for him to become aware of words and ideas. Books stir the child's curiosity, introduce him to new information and concepts, enlarge his vocabulary, and increase his attention span. When an adult reads a book to a child, he has a wonderful opportunity to share with the child and show love to him.

Young children like to look at pictures in books. They are attracted by the bright colors and will often name what they see. They are able to answer simple questions about the picture.

Older children enjoy books with a simple story of around 150 or more words. When you select books, choose those in which the words have been used in a captivating way. "The bed squeaked. The floor squeaked. The leaves fell on the roof. Swish. Swish. The teakettle whistled. Hiss. Hiss."[2] Preschoolers love a book in which ideas are rhythmically expressed, repeated, and built up. Some fours and fives will recognize a few words on the page and will want to tell you about this.

Books for children should describe things with which they are familiar—family activities, pets, and daily experiences. They should portray right conduct and introduce the child to concepts about God and Jesus. For young children, choose books with large, bright pictures and only a few words on the page. Also, feel free to change the words to relate to the concept you are teaching. For example, a book that contains pictures to match alphabet letters is very good. Point to the picture of the apple and ask the child what it is. When he tells you, say, "God made the apple." You can do this for almost any picture in the book.

Nature Corner. When a preschooler sees and handles objects from nature, he has the opportunity to learn many things about God. He learns that God created the world and everything in it. He discovers that God made things to be beautiful, soft, cuddly, or good smelling. He begins to understand that God is loving, caring, and very wise. The teacher has many opportunities to teach through guided conversation as the child interacts with nature objects.

Some care needs to be exercised in the use of nature objects with young preschoolers. Their first tendency is to pick up the item and then to put it into their mouths. Some plants can be poisonous. Follow the suggestions given in your curriculum materials for selecting nature items.

Children also need to be supervised in caring for nature items. Watering plants will be so much fun that they may drown them. Fish may receive so much food that they die of overeating.

Older preschoolers can enjoy simple experiments with nature objects. Rather than answering a child's questions directly, help the child discover his answer for himself. Children who are helped to plant and water seeds will learn about the miracle of growth. Older preschoolers can also learn what happens to plants that do not receive light or water. As they do, their appreciation for God's wisdom in providing these things will grow, and their trust in Him increase.

Art Activities. No other medium offers the child so many varied opportunities to learn and grow. The kinds of art activities you may use with preschoolers are almost endless. All of them teach the child valuable lessons in self-expression, learning about materials, sharing, and creating. When a child is allowed to use art materials freely, he not only learns about the properties of those materials, but he feels the sense of accomplishment which comes from creating.

Children pass through various stages in their use of materials. At first, they only want to manipulate them. They will squeeze and pound the clay, smear the paste, or run their fingers through the beans or other collage items. These activities do not seem very purposeful or productive to adults; but they are. Through them, the child is learning what the material is like. Through guided conversation, the child's activity may be related to spiritual truth—"God gave you hands to squeeze the clay. Thank You, God, for hands."

Later, the child will begin to control the materials better. He will draw a line up or down on the page with the crayon. He learns that he can stick two objects together with paste. He makes interesting designs with the beans.

Fours and fives begin to use the materials to make something specific, such as a picture or an object. They also like to talk about what they are creating, giving it a name. The object or picture may not look much like what the child says it is; but this is his perception of what he has done, and it should be accepted by the teacher.

Art activities are very soothing to children. At a camp meeting, 100 preschoolers were jammed together in a small room for 2½ hours. In desperation, the leaders finally had them sit down at tables and gave each child a lump of clay about the size of a plum. For 45 minutes, the two- to five-year-old children, who were tired and had been crying, quietly rolled, pounded, squeezed, and manipulated the clay. Younger children merely manipulated it. Older ones made baskets and snakes. But all found release and relaxation as they used the material.

Art activities also help a child to express what he has learned and to share his ideas with others. For example, a child can use construction paper to tear objects for a "day and night" picture. Through guided conversation, the teacher can help the child remember that "God made day for play and night for rest." She can commend a child for his interesting use of materials, and relate this to the way he is growing, or to the abilities God has given him.

The important thing to remember about preschool art projects is that the process is more important to the child than the product. His learning comes through using the materials creatively. He is not concerned about the neatness of the finished product. For this reason, adults should absolutely refrain from doctoring up a child's picture or object.

Music. Music can be used in many ways to teach preschoolers. For babies, music is very soothing. Sing or croon to a young child to quiet him or rock him to sleep.

For toddlers and older children, use music to teach concepts about God, express thanks to God, interpret a shared respond better to a song instruction—"Let's pick up toys and put them all away"—than to a verbal command. In addition to these informal uses of music, use singing as a part of the large-group time for older preschoolers.

Although all children enjoy music, they respond differently to it. Younger preschoolers will simply watch and listen while you sing to them. This can be frustrating to an inexperienced teacher who wants the children to sing along. Remember, that although they are not singing, they are learning. Threes may begin to sing with you and to imitate you in an action song or finger play. Fours and fives are more accomplished in singing as a group. They also enjoy small-group activities with an Autoharp and rhythm instruments.

Songs for children need to be selected carefully. Words should describe concrete experiences with which the children are familiar, and be scripturally and doctrinally sound. Ideas should be kept simple with only one main idea in a song for toddlers and twos and threes. Children also love songs that use their names. One teacher used the song "I have a helper; Jimmy is his name" to commend a child who was doing something helpful or kind.

When children are getting wiggly and restless, music helps to relax them. Action songs that involve bending, stretching, and other movements, help them to use their wiggles creatively and in a purposeful manner.

Prayer. Dr. Mary LeBar emphasizes the importance of teaching even very young children to pray aloud, so that they will not feel hesitation to do this later on. Preschoolers should think of prayer as talking to God, similar to the way they talk with parents and teachers. No special prayer posture is necessary. Instead, as the child takes part in informal activities, the teacher can guide his thoughts to prayer. For example, "Thank You, God, for the pretty flower," at the nature center; or "Thank You, God, for good food," at the home-living center. Prayers with children need to be simple, often expressing just one thought in words that a child would use. Otherwise, the prayer does not really represent a religious experience that is natural to him.

With older preschoolers include prayer as part of the large-group experience. Let the children talk about things for which to pray, and guide them to use many forms of prayer: prayers asking forgiveness, prayers of thanks to God, and prayers for the needs of themselves and others.

In Conclusion

The above discussion of methods is by no means exhaustive; it only suggests some of the many things you can do to teach preschoolers effectively. For more complete details on how to teach preschoolers, consult the curriculum materials provided for the various preschool ministries.

REFERENCE NOTES

1. Information on nursery rooms and equipment was adapted from *Living and Learning with Nursery Children,* by Joy Latham (Kansas City: Beacon Hill Press of Kansas City, 1975), pp. 80-96.

2. Ann McGovern, *Too Much Noise* (New York: Scholastic Book Services, 1967), p. 32.

Dear Teacher,
When I look into your eyes
And search deep into your heart,
Shall I find something beautiful
  About my face,
  About my being?

YOUR PUPIL

5

Ministering to Elementary Children

"Children are an heritage of the Lord," wrote Solomon (Ps. 127:3, KJV), and how right he was. Children represent the future of the church. How important it is, then, to minister to their needs today so they can become strong, committed Christians who, as they grow to maturity, will live for the Lord and reach out to others. To do this, we must know something about the characteristics of children ages 6 through 11. Only as we understand what they are like—how they think and act—can we hope to teach them in ways that will make a significant difference in their lives.

In this chapter, we will look at the characteristics of children. We will then consider the space and equipment requirements for elementary children. Following this, we will discuss learning activities and methodology appropriate to primary, middler, and junior children.

Characteristics of Primaries—6-7 years

PHYSICAL

Has attained about two-thirds of adult height.

Growing unevenly. Heart growing slower than rest of body. Fatigues easily but revives quickly.

Needs alternate periods of activity and quiet to avoid overfatigue. May resist rest.

Susceptible to various childhood diseases.

Large muscles developing rapidly, faster than small muscles.

Large-muscle development causes child to be restless and always on the move. Child wiggles, jumps, twists, and turns incessantly.

Loves to run and chase.

Loves to do, rather than just watch and listen.

Loves activity for its own sake. Activity does not need to be purposeful.

Finer muscles developing, but more slowly than large.

Coordination of large and fine muscles improving.

Beginning to use scissors and crayons with more skill.

Loves to cut, paste, and fold paper.

Eyes not fully developed; may be farsighted. Eye-hand coordination may not be good in young primaries.

Should not be required to do detail work for long periods of time. Crafts and handwork must be simple.

MENTAL

Learning to read and write. Likes to use these new skills. Beginning to see relationships between written and spoken words.

Vocabulary increasing. Likes to try new and big words. May also like vulgar words and "shock" words.

Likes word and number games.

Attention span about 7-10 minutes.

Eager to learn. Asks questions. Wants to know "why." Curious. Believes what he is told. Believes adults are generally right.

Learns best through senses.

Just beginning to reason and draw conclusions.

Ideas need to be kept simple. Introduce only one new idea at a time.

Has trouble making decisions by himself. Needs help and practice in problem solving.

Growing in ability to distinguish fact from fantasy. Does not understand concepts of time, space, and distance. Lives in the here and now.

Thinks literally. Does not understand symbolism. Has good imagination. May have an imaginary friend. Loves dramatic play.

Can memorize easily. Enjoys and learns from repetition.

EMOTIONAL

Emotions near surface. Laughs and cries easily. Emotions change often.

Easily embarrassed or excited. Reflects these in bodily movements.

May withdraw to escape pressure or embarrassment. Sevens may be introspective and thoughtful.

Many fears—of dentist, new experiences, dark, being lost, or change.

Worries, especially sevens. Worries about home problems, possible failure, etc. Often cautious.

Wants new experiences, but needs the security of home.

Feels secure in familiar routines.

Wants to be grown-up and independent, but finds mature behavior difficult.

Sets high standards for self. Wants to be perfect. "Eraser" years. Impatient with self and with others. Needs praise and encouragement in order to cope with lack of ability to be perfect.	May resent demands on self. May threaten to run away. Can empathize with others who are sad or lonely. Good time to encourage these feelings.
SOCIAL Moving out from home to school. Loves parties, but may not behave well. Likes to play with children, but wants to be the center of attention. Likes group games, but wants to be leader or "it." May refuse to play if he cannot be first. Just beginning to move from "I" to "we." Not ready for much competition. Very poor loser. Wants children for friends, but friendships may be short-lived and change often. Beginning to defend self with words as well as by physical fighting.	Likes to talk. Respects authority. Believes that adults are right. If he sees an adult doing something wrong, has a hard time believing that it really is wrong. Wants praise and encouragement from teachers and other adults. Loves to be a helper of adults. Sensitive to criticism from adults. Believes adults can be trusted. Likes to collect. Legalistic. Wants fairness and justice. Hard to understand concepts of grace and mercy. Does not understand "bending" of rules.
SPIRITUAL Likes Sunday school. Wants to see teacher and friends. Likes Bible stories. Likes to take part in Sunday school activities. Growing rapidly in concepts of God. Feels relationship to God. Can feel separation from God when he does wrong. Feels secure in God's love and care. Loves nature and relates this to God. Loves Jesus. Thinks of Him as a Friend and Helper. Prays with faith and conviction. May have	trouble understanding why God does not answer prayer the way he wants. Curious about death and heaven. Wants to be good. Understands difference between good and bad, true and untrue, right and wrong. Concept of good closely tied to reward and punishment; but growing in concept of good as being what significant adults in his life approve (or disapprove) of. Has trouble admitting personal wrongdoing. Alibis often. May be ready for salvation.

Characteristics of Middlers—8-9 Years

PHYSICAL

Slow, steady growth. Grows 2-3 inches and 3-6 pounds per year.
Movements swift, skillful, and refined.
Eye-hand coordination improving. Can cut and write with skill. Likes to copy and do uncomplicated craft activities.
Large muscles still developing. Still needs and likes physical activity. Often runs, jumps, drums with fingers, etc.
Likes to do things.

Likes to develop physical skills. Practices skills over and over to perfect them.
Enjoys organized group games. Likes to be out of doors.
Generally healthy and resistant to fatigue. May have some difficulty calming down after long period of strenuous activity.
Accident prone because he moves so quickly and tends to overestimate abilities.
Likes a physical challenge.

MENTAL

Reading and writing skills well developed in some. Begins to use cursive writing.
Those who read and write well enjoy using skills to look up information and find facts for themselves.
Able to work independently better than younger child. Works long and hard on projects that interest him.
Often does not hear directions because he is eager to begin activity.
Communicates well. Loves to talk and discuss.

Curious; asks many questions.
Memorizes easily.
Understands time, space, and distance better than younger child. Ready for simple chronology and simple maps.
Can organize and classify. Able to rank order five to seven items.
Reasons mentally, but only about the concrete and real.
Still thinks quite literally. Does not understand symbolism.

SOCIAL

Area of rapid development. Child's world expands to school and community as well as home.
Wants acceptance and approval of peers. This is more important than approval of adults.
Tends to have special friend and special enemy of same age and sex.
Loyal as a friend. Able to play with friends with less fighting.

Boys and girls beginning to separate in interests and activities; do not like to do things together except in groups.
Clubs and gangs beginning to form.
Pulling away from adults, but need subtle adult guidance.
Well aware of values of significant adults, even though he is pulling away from adults.
Beginning to be a hero-worshiper.

EMOTIONAL

Outgoing and friendly. Less introspective than at seven.
Beginning to gain self-awareness and respect as he interacts with other children.
Often impatient. Says, "I can't wait till . . ."
Reaching out to others. Concerned about the rights of others, and about fairness.
Emotions sometimes up and down.

May experience feelings of inadequacy or inferiority.
Fewer fears than as a primary.
Worries a lot. Worries about failure and not being accepted.
Resents criticism from adults.
Curious about the world, current events, and the past.

SPIRITUAL

Generally enjoys Sunday school, if it is interesting.

May have questions about the reality of God if he once believed in Santa and now knows this is a fairy tale.

Prays earnestly and in faith about anything and everything.

Knows the difference between fact and fantasy, right and wrong.

Beginning to make ethical decisions based on his understanding of right and wrong.

Ready to be taught all basic Bible truths on child's level. Spiritual truth needs to be taught concretely.

Some are ready for conversion.

Enjoys owning and reading his personal Bible.

Characteristics of Juniors—10-11 Years

PHYSICAL

Slow, steady growth at age 10; may experience growth spurt near end of 11th year.

Some may enter puberty. Girls growing faster than boys.

Beginning to look more like an adult.

Healthy, but accident prone. Recovers quickly from injuries. Past most childhood diseases.

Able to care for physical needs, but does not care much about appearance.

Full of energy. Likes games and activities that require coordination and skill. Has good coordination.

Noisy. Loves to scuffle, tease, and sometimes fight.

Would rather talk, read, or listen than work.

Loves adventure out of doors.

MENTAL

Curious, eager to learn. Wants to know reasons. Not satisfied with pat answers.

May be disenchanted with school. Resents rigorous work and limits on freedom; but still wants to learn.

Peak reading age.

Many interests. Likes to experiment and to collect.

Vocabulary has doubled since he entered school.

Able to take responsibility.

Attention span is 15-20 minutes.

Good memory.

Growing concepts of space, time, and distance.

Still thinks concretely, but moving toward ability to think abstractly and symbolically. Enjoys reasoning things out for himself.

Reasonable. Accepts logical conclusions.

Likes to collect.

Likes to make things.

Able to take responsibility for planning and carrying out projects.

SOCIAL

Strong desire to be part of group. May lie or steal rather than be ostracized by peers.

Loyal to peers. Likes to belong to gangs or clubs.

Pulling away from adults. May use slang or dirty talk to assert independence from adults.

Resents authority over him.

A hero-worshiper. Likes hero stories.

Rivalry, but some interest, between sexes. Boys and girls want to be separate for most activities. Can work together in groups.

Enjoys competition.

Demands fairness and justice.

If adult likes child, child returns love and is loyal.

EMOTIONAL

Good control of emotions in public. Even at home is beginning to express emotion in acceptable ways.

Ten is a stable, happy, cooperative age. Elevens may be moody and less stable.

Dislikes outward display of affection.

Can be cruel to others at times, but also growing in concern for others. Concerned about fairness.

Enthusiastic about projects and activities.

Enjoys humor, especially slapstick. Sense of humor may overflow at inappropriate times.

Few fears.

SPIRITUAL

Age of spiritual readiness.

Asks many questions about spiritual matters. Wants reality in spiritual life.

Often ready for salvation.

Can be helped to develop Christian habits.

Wants to contribute to the church. May be ready for church membership.

Has a "doing" rather than a "feeling" faith.

Sets high standards for himself and tries to live up to them.

Prayer becoming more personal.

ENVIRONMENT, ROOMS, FURNISHINGS, AND MATERIALS

A Good Learning Environment for Children

Children are sensitive to their surroundings. A room that is drab, dark, cluttered, or overcrowded does not invite pupils to an exciting adventure in learning. Nor does it say to them, "This is God's house—a special place I should respect."

Children may not analyze or express their feelings about their rooms; but they are sure to make their reactions known in various ways, some of which may be annoying to adults. Sometimes, children are affected by things of which we are not aware. Rooms that are too brightly colored overstimulate children and tend to make them boisterous and unruly. Rooms where nothing is soundproof have the same effect.

Very few rooms will be perfect according to some "ideal" standard. However, they can all be made cheerful and kept neat and clean. Concerned children's workers who are aware of the ideal can constantly work toward it as time, space, and finances become available.

Rooms for Elementary Children

Space and Location. Children learn best by doing. Therefore, space must be provided for a variety of activities, both large- and small-group. In addition, an open, spacious room has a good psychological effect on children. Classes for elementary children need to provide 25-30 square feet per pupil. Assign the larger rooms to younger children. The maximum number of pupils in a room should be 30. When the number exceeds that, plan to break into smaller classes and departments. If you have an assembly room flanked by individual classrooms, provide at least 8-10 square feet of space per pupil in the assembly area.

As you are selecting rooms for children, also consider the amount of unbroken wall space available. This space is needed for bulletin boards, chalkboards, picture rails, and for storing large pieces of equipment.

If possible, locate children's rooms near an outside entrance, rest rooms, and a drinking fountain. Each classroom should have a door which opens on to a hall corridor.

Walls, Windows, and Floors. Classroom walls and ceilings should be soundproof. Use acoustical tile on the ceiling. Paint walls with washable paint in soft colors. If ceilings are low, paint or tile them in a lighter shade than the walls. This gives the effect of height. If they are high, use the same color as the walls to make them appear lower.

In dark rooms, or rooms with a northern exposure, shades of yellow, buff, or soft rose add warmth. Blues, grays, and greens are best for rooms with a lot of sunshine.

Because of the colorful pictures, bulletin boards, posters, and creative work which should always be on display in children's rooms, plain walls are better than decorated ones. Touches of bright color may be used for accent, but restrict this to small areas.

Try to have windows on one-fifth or one-fourth of the room's wall space. Windows should be low enough for pupils to see out. If drapes are used, they should be fairly plain and should not obstruct the view or the light (unless the room is too sunny). Shades or venetian blinds allow the room to be darkened for showing audiovisuals.

Floors should have a sturdy covering which can be easily and thoroughly cleaned. Carpet is an excellent buy. It is more expensive than tile or paint; but it reduces noise and makes more effective use of the floor. When choosing carpet, stick to plain colors and materials which can be cleaned.

Furnishing the Room

The furnishings placed in an elementary classroom are of great importance. They need to be sturdy, comfortable for the children, and useful in helping them to explore and learn. Here are some needed items.

Chairs. These should be sturdy, but light enough in weight for the children to move them about easily. This is especially important when space is at a premium. Provide only enough chairs for your expected attendance, plus one or two extras for visitors. Pupils can move chairs from large-group to small-group activities, rather than having duplicate chairs.

Chairs should be built to support the small of the back as well as the shoulders. A plain wood finish, varnished and waxed, will give years of service; however, painted or colored plastic chairs are also attractive. When purchasing new chairs, select nonfolding chairs which can be stacked.

Chair seats for primaries should be 12 inches from the floor, for middlers 14 inches, and for juniors 16 inches. If you have only primary (grades one to three) and junior (grades four to six) groups, use 12-inch chairs for primaries and 16-inch chairs for juniors.

Tables. Rectangular tables are most useful in the classroom. They should be 10 inches higher than the chairs, and have tops about 30 inches wide. In a small room, use tables that are 30" x 48"; in larger rooms tables can be 30" x 54" or 30" x 60". Select tables with corner legs.

If you have limited space for tables, shelves attached to the wall may do as a substitute. These should be hinged so they will fold flat against the wall when not in use.

Try to provide one or more small tables for the worship center, growing plants, and learning centers. However, do not fill the room with tables; space is more important.

Shelves. You need both open shelves, for pupils' materials and supplies, and a cabinet for teachers' materials. Pupils' shelves should be about 42 inches high, 3 feet wide, with shelves that are 14 inches deep with 12-14 inches of space between the shelves. This provides adequate storage for record players, construction paper, and other supplies. Shelves should have a closed back.

If space is at a premium, the teacher's cabinet can be attached to the wall. Try to make it large enough for storing items such as poster board.

Chalkboard, Tackboard, and Picture Rail. On one or more sides of the room, provide tackboards (made of corkboard or wallboard) and a chalkboard. Try to provide a ratio of 3 feet of tackboard to 1 foot of chalkboard. For primaries and middlers, 6 feet of chalkboard and 18 feet of tackboard is good; for juniors, try to provide 8 feet of chalkboard and 24 feet of tackboard. Boards should be about 30 inches high and 28 inches from the floor. Along the bottom, place a chalk tray or picture rail. This provides space to display pictures and posters the children make, as well as pictures the teacher uses.

Musical Instruments. A studio-size piano is useful for elementary departments but is not an absolute necessity. It should be kept in good tune, with all keys working.

If a piano is not available, use an Autoharp or ChromAharP. A record player and/or cassette tape recorder is also excellent. Children can learn to sing very well with taped or recorded accompaniment. These tools also make possible a variety of classroom music activities, such as listening to music or recorded Bible stories.

Coatrack. If no coatrack is available in the department or a nearby hall, place a shelf at the back or side of the room. It should be about four and a half feet from the floor, with hooks underneath for wraps. As a safety precaution, be sure the hooks are above the children's eye level.

Permanent Pictures. One or two carefully selected framed pictures may be hung for permanent display. They should be religious pictures and should be hung at the eye level of the children. The pictures which come in the teaching resource packets are often suitable for framing. If your picture frame has a removable back, you can change the pictures from time to time.

In Addition. Workers in children's departments need to have access to a variety of audiovisual equipment, such as overhead projectors and slide, film, and filmstrip projectors. Although very few churches can afford to purchase this type of equipment for every department, it should be available in a central location for teachers to check out and use. A church resource center is an excellent solution for this situation. There teachers can find not only the AVs they need, but other helpful materials such as teaching supplies (paper, pencils, etc.), picture files, bulletin board helps, Bible games, cutting boards, and laminating equipment (either professional or rolls of clear, self-adhesive plastic). When a church sets up a resource center, teachers can exercise good stewardship by helping each other make supplementary teaching items and by sharing both supplies and equipment. A resource center also provides a good storage area for use by all children's workers.

Materials and Supplies

In addition to the basic equipment items already discussed, an elementary classroom needs to have a wealth of supplies and materials which teachers and pupils can use for Bible study and creative Bible learning activities. Curriculum materials for the various children's ministries contain detailed lists of the specific items needed. Here are some general items you will want to provide.

☐ Bibles. Have both a large-print department Bible and a few copies of a good-quality King James Version student Bible. Although we encourage pupils to bring their Bibles to church, not all of them do so. Also, pupils often bring Bibles of many different versions. These are excellent for study and understanding; but since most Nazarene curriculum materials are based on the use of the King James Version, pupils need access to it.

☐ Literature. This is a must for workers. At the end of this book's chapters on Sunday and weekday ministries and at the end of each section delineated in the chapter on annual and special ministries are lists of the curriculum resources provided by the Nazarene Publishing House. Make these available to workers.

☐ Books. Provide books for children and books for workers. The curriculum materials for the various ministries suggest books that will be helpful.

☐ Music Books. Two new books are now available to use in children's work. In most cases, the books are needed only by teachers, song directors, and pianists, not by the children. For juniors, however, it is wise to provide a songbook for every one or two children. The names of the songbooks are: *Songs of God and Me* and *Sing!*

☐ Nature Materials. These add beauty to the classroom and also teach children many things about God. Try to provide both seasonal items, which you or the children bring in, and more permanent ones, such as an aquarium, a terrarium, or potted plants.

☐ Creative Art Supplies. Provide crayons; paste and glue; scissors; pencils; rulers; felt markers in various sizes and colors; construction, newsprint, and manila paper; clay or dough; tempera paint and brushes; transparent and masking tape; thumbtacks or pushpins; and paper clips.

☐ Maps, Charts, and "Nu-Vu" Backgrounds. Complete sets of these are provided for primaries, middlers, and juniors. Order the set described in your age-level curriculum material.

What Can You Do When Things Aren't Exactly Perfect?

Miss Miller looked with dismay at the room to which she had been assigned to teach primary children. It was located in an old inner-city house. Although there were several large windows, they were dirty. The drab brown and gold wallpaper and the tattered shades further served to darken the room. A naked lightbulb graced a stained and cracked ceiling. The dingy rug—obviously a product of the Victorian era—only partially covered a gray painted floor which was badly chipped. The room contained a sturdy table and chairs in the correct size, but they nearly filled the area. The rest of the furnishings consisted of rickety tables and cabinets, left over from the days when the house had been an apartment building. The room was small—perhaps large enough to use for 5 or 6 pupils at most. Miss Miller's enrollment was 12. Worst of all, the church served a poor community. There was almost no money for regular expenses, let alone classroom repairs and refurbishment.

Obviously, this is an extreme picture of an inadequate learning situation; but such rooms do exist. Even in churches where the problem is not quite so critical, workers often have to struggle with (1) lack of space, (2) inappropriate furnishings, (3) inadequate supplies, (4) a limited budget for changing these things, or, worst of all, (5) all of the above.

What can be done in such situations? Is it possible to provide good Christian education when rooms and materials are less than—perhaps far from—perfect? The answer is yes, if leaders and workers are willing to exercise their imaginations, make some sacrifices, and work hard to improve the situation. Here are just a few things that can be done.

☐ Begin with real commitment to the idea that children's work deserves high priority. With this in mind, look at the way the church budget is being spent. Perhaps there are other areas where expenses could be trimmed to provide more money for the needs of the Children's Department.

☐ Do all you can with soap, water, and possibly paint. These (except for paint) are your least expensive commodities. No matter what a room is like otherwise, it can be clean and neat.

☐ Decide what can be touched up or covered up. Could men in the church reinforce the wobbly tables? saw off legs on equipment that is too large for children? paint or paper with at least reasonable skill? Can the women sew attractive coverings for unsightly cabinets or table surfaces? Miss Miller, for example, covered one table with a piece of wine-colored velveteen. The result? A beautiful Bible table.

☐ When space is limited, (1) divide the class, or (2) make more room in the class. Dividing a class is a good way to start, since this will tend to promote growth in the department. But if no room is available for another class, look at what is in an overcrowded room. A massive piano can be the first thing to go. Use record players, tape recorders, or other instruments in its place. Look for smaller tables. Consider using the floor (if it is clean) for some activities. Move furniture around during the session, as needed. One teacher was faced with the problem of a massive table which had been built inside the classroom. It could not be removed without chopping it to bits because it was too large to go through the door. His solution? Each week, pupils helped him to move the table back and forth to make space in the room when it was needed.

☐ Keep on display only the things which relate to the current unit of study or current activities. Cluttered rooms look even more crowded than they are. Keep pictures and displays to a minimum in this situation. File or get rid of items not actively in use.

☐ If cabinets are not available, store materials in cardboard boxes in which you have cut handles. These boxes should have lids and be labeled. If groups share a room, each one should have separate boxes for items not shared and should remove their supplies after their period in the room.

☐ If bulletin boards or chalkboards are not available, you can purchase cardboard trifolds from the Nazarene Publishing House. These can be used for displays or learning center dividers by just setting them on a table. Also available is a combination chalkboard and felt board.

☐ Whatever you do, do not let problems like these deter you from doing your best for children. And remember—the room and its furnishings are only part of the story in children's ministry. More important to the total learning environment are the workers themselves.

METHODS—
WAYS THE ELEMENTARY SCHOOL CHILD LEARNS

Not long ago, in a Sunday school workshop for teachers of elementary school children, a conference participant commented on the information which had just been presented. "I just love all these good ideas," he said. "But I don't know what to do. By the time I have presented the lesson, there is no time left for activities like this."

Unfortunately, many sincere Christian teachers of children have a similar lack of understanding about the methods they should use to teach children. They view the "lesson" as the telling of the Bible story, followed by a period of working in the workbook. Then if there is time—and there never is—they might try a Bible game, creative drama, or art activity. Activities like these are looked upon something like the frosting on a cake—nice but not essential.

The fact is, however, that boys and girls need to be active learners. When they simply sit and listen, they are likely to retain only about 10 percent of what they hear. When they are actively involved in Bible learning activities, they will retain about 90 percent of what they do.

A method is simply a way of getting something done. In the Sunday school, a teacher's method is his way of presenting information and/or guiding pupils in active Bible learning. Sometimes the teacher takes the most active role—for example, when a story is told. Even then, however, the wise teacher plans to involve the pupils. When he tells a story, he may divide pupils into listening teams and assign each team a question to answer or an idea to look for. At other times, the teacher's method is to provide a pupil activity during which the pupil takes the leading role in his learning. This kind of method is known as a creative Bible learning activity. The teacher is involved in the outworking of the project; but his role is that of a guide to learning, rather than just a giver of information. He helps the pupils plan, clarifies ideas, and sometimes presents information; but the pupils are the ones who carry out the project.

Bible learning activities are not just extras to use to fill the few moments before the class bell rings. They are a means of guiding boys and girls to discover and apply Bible truths. They do not come after the lesson—they are part of the lesson. Let's take a close look at some of the kinds of creative Bible learning activities that can be used effectively to teach spiritual truths.

The word *creative* is one that frightens many teachers. They immediately conjure up images of Michelangelo, C. S. Lewis, or Enrico Caruso. However, as Elsiebeth McDaniel has said, "Every person has the capacity for creativity. It is not, as some may think, the private possession of just a few. When creativity is nurtured, it grows. When it is neglected, it may disappear."[1]

Webster's defines *create* in this way: "cause; make; to produce through imaginative skill." *Creative* is described as "productive." These definitions help to remove some of the mystery and terror associated with the word, for we see that many of the things which we normally do can be described as creative. The housewife who adds a special garnish to a dish of food is being creative; so is the child who draws a picture of something he has learned or experienced. In the process of creation, the person uses his imagination to combine the old with the new in a way that is unique and different.

A creative Bible activity, then, is one in which the child participates actively and through which he has a productive, firsthand experience. Creative activities are important to Bible learning because they require the pupil to do something more than just sit and listen. Through some he explores and discovers Bible truths; through others he expresses what he has learned. But in all of them, the child has the opportunity to use a variety of tools to learn in a fresh, new way.

Bible learning activities are important, too, because they provide for individual differences in children. Some children enjoy drawing pictures; others hate it. Some boys and girls are especially gifted at writing or reading; others love to assemble a bulletin board. When the teacher provides some options of activity, each child can learn by doing something he enjoys.

It is important to remember, however, that even though Bible learning activities make learning enjoyable, they should never be used just to entertain the child or to keep him busy. Each activity should have a definite purpose related to the lesson being studied.

As you plan a learning activity, ask, "What is my learning goal? What do I want the pupils to know—to feel—to do?"

When you have answered these questions, you are ready to consider which Bible learning activity will help you accomplish your goal. Each activity you select should help pupils to (1) learn new Bible facts or ideas; (2) memorize Bible verses; (3) learn to use the Bible; or (4) relate Bible truths to life.

The variety of learning activities available to use in teaching the Bible is nearly inexhaustible; however, most activities can be placed in one of these groups: art, drama, writing, books and research, oral communication, Bible games, and music; Bible memorization should also be included.

Bible Learning Through Creative Art

Creative art is perhaps one of the most varied and satisfying Bible learning activities for children. Not only does art provide them with an opportunity for expression of ideas and thoughts, but it also meets their need for activity in learning.

Through creative artwork, children can (1) learn new facts and ideas through the discussion and research which precedes the activity, (2) learn to plan and work together, (3) grow in the ability to think and make decisions, (4) grow in the confidence that comes from thinking and creating, and (5) express ideas and understandings of important facts and principles.

Creative art is not mere busywork, just to give pupils something to do. Rather, it is the Bible research, related discussion, and, finally, the expression of learning which are most important. Art activities can be used to illustrate what a pupil has learned about a Bible story, Bible verse, or a life-related concept. Some art projects can be used to experience a biblical concept. For example, pupils can make a booklet or Bible game to give to a sick friend. Through this experience, they are led to live out the Bible command to "love one another" (John 13:34).

Art activities are also good study-starters. For example, in a lesson on being kind to others, pupils could draw pictures to show how they feel when others are not kind to them. From this art project, the teacher has a natural discussion point from which she may lead the pupils into the Bible study. After the study, artwork could be used to help pupils express various ways of showing kindness to others.

Many times people refer to art-related Bible activities as

"crafts." However, there are several important differences. A craft activity is one in which the end product is the most significant reason for the activity. A child usually learns some skills as he makes the craft; but his motive for participating in the activity is simply to make something. In Bible learning activity, the end product is seldom really important once the activity has been completed (except when it is to be used as a gift). The emphasis is on the Bible facts, verses, or truths the pupil will learn, the research he must do, and the choices he makes. The product made during the activity—such as a mural, booklet, or collage—is only the means to the end, or the means of expressing what has been learned.

This important fact tells us something about the way we should react to the child's work. In a craft, we strive for skill development and as much perfection as possible in the end product; but in a Bible learning activity, we are much less concerned about this. We want children to work neatly and carefully, but even a child who is not a very good artist can use artwork to illustrate the meaning of a Bible verse. In our evaluation of the child's success, we do not look at his art ability. Rather, we check to see what growth in knowledge, attitudes, or behavior changes he has demonstrated through the project experience.

Be bold to experiment with art activities as a means of helping pupils learn. Far too many teachers are content to use only one method and one medium—drawing pictures using crayons or felt markers. Children, especially middlers and juniors, will soon tire of artwork that is mostly drawing and coloring. Consider these other possibilities.

Booklets
Charts and posters
Collages—pictures or designs with three-dimensional objects
Dioramas—three-dimensional scenes in a small box
Displays and exhibits
Friezes—a series of scenes related to one subject
Maps
Mobiles
Model making
Montages—pictures made by overlapping other pictures or words

Murals—one long scene about a single subject

Picture making—through painting, drawing, paper cutting
  or tearing

Illustrated time-lines

Consider, too, using materials other than paper and crayons. Try: construction paper, cloth, rickrack and other sewing trims, poster paint, clay, and actual objects for collages.

Bible Learning Through Creative Drama

Because the stories of the Bible are written so briefly and succinctly, it is sometimes difficult to feel the full impact of the emotions and struggles which Bible people experienced; yet children need this understanding in order to adequately relate the Bible to their own life needs. Creative drama is one way to make Bible characters seem real and to bring the Bible to life.

Often when we think of drama, we think of a well-practiced, highly polished performance. Creative drama is different, however. The value is not in the final performance but in the experience the child has as he is enacting a Bible story or life-related situation.

Through creative drama, pupils are helped to get inside the skin of another person, to relive the events of that person's life. Through drama the child can experience the meaning of such concepts as love, kindness, sharing, or forgiveness. He can express his understanding of important ideas and gain skill in solving life problems. Through drama a teacher can learn much about his pupils. Drama also helps the pupils gain a better appreciation for the feelings and ideas of others.

Successful drama begins and ends with Bible or life-related study and discussion. For example, before a child can act out a Bible story, he must first become thoroughly familiar with it—through hearing or reading it and through thought-provoking discussion. This discussion helps pupils to get the facts in mind and to compare Bible people with themselves and realize what their thoughts and feelings were in various situations.

There are many types of dramatic activity, ranging from choral readings or speaking, to dramatizing a Bible or life-related story. However, the steps for guiding children in drama are very much the same for many of them—especially story play, picture posing, picture drama, and role play. These steps are:

1. Tell the story or describe the life-related situation.
2. Discuss the story or situation. Consider all the facts; then talk about the feelings of the characters involved. If you are dramatizing a scene in a teaching picture, name the characters in the picture.
3. Ask for volunteers to take the parts and act out the situation. No script is needed. Pupils will make up conversation based on their understanding of the situation and (in role play) its solution.
4. For the players, briefly redescribe the story events or life-related problem situation.
5. Allow players to do the dramatization.
6. Evaluate the drama. In a Bible story drama, decide whether players accurately portrayed the characters. In a role play, discuss the feelings and the solutions that were presented.
7. Reenact the scene, using different characters, one or more times as time permits and interest continues. Relate the drama to Bible truths under consideration for that day.

When you first begin to use drama, you may find that the children are embarrassed and get silly or giggly. Don't allow this reaction to stop you from using drama. Help the pupils overcome their feelings by keeping the focus of attention on the problem situation or the Bible story. Usually after a few tries children lose their sense of embarrassment. Simple puppets and costumes add interest to dramatic activities. Puppets can be made quickly from paper plates, paper bags, or even *Nu-Vu* figures attached to Popsicle sticks or straws. Often a shy child feels better about participating in a drama when he has a puppet to use.

Effective drama activities for children include:

Choral Reading—pupils divide a Bible passage, poem, or story into separate parts and read them with expression which helps to interpret the passage.

Puppet Drama

Story Drama

Dramatic Interview—pupils study a Bible passage as a story. One person is chosen to be interviewed; the others create questions for that person to answer. When interviewed, the one representing the character must answer as he thinks that person would have.

Pantomime—drama without words in which players act with body movements and gestures only.

Picture Drama—children act out a situation which is suggested by a scene in a picture. Dialogue is used.

Picture Posing—children take the body positions and facial expressions of characters shown in a picture. No dialogue is involved.

Role Play—drama about real-life situations. The player takes the part of another person, speaking and acting as he thinks that person would.

Tableau—drama which is like a still picture. As children enact the scene, a narrator reads or music is provided.

Two cautions need to be observed in using drama with children. First, in Bible story plays it is better not to let a child take the part of Jesus. Instead, display a picture and let a good reader (or the teacher) read His words.

Second, in role play do not cast a child in a role which is too similar to his personality. Instead, let the loud child take the part of a quiet, shy individual. To cast a person in a role "too close to home" may embarrass him or cause an emotional upheaval.

Bible Learning Through Creative Writing

The ability to restate an idea in one's own words is one of the clearest indications that learning has taken place. Writing activities also let children express personal feelings and thoughts. Because of this, writing activities can be used in many ways and for many purposes. Here are just a few.

- Newspaper stories may be written to summarize and interpret Bible stories. The Bible study which the pupil does before writing makes the story more meaningful.

- A poem or paragraph can be written to express a pupil's feelings and ideas.

- Short stories give pupils an opportunity to tell how problem situations could be resolved.

- Charts and posters help pupils summarize their learning.

- Letters may be written to express appreciation to another person.

As with art projects, writing activities may be used to lead up to the Bible study or to recall and reinforce what has been learned. For example, before a story, pupils might read an open-ended story describing a problem situation, and write down how they would feel or what they would do in that situation. This activity provides the springboard discussion to lead into the Bible story or study. After the Bible study, pupils might write stories summarizing the Bible content, or perhaps rewrite their solutions to the problem situation.

Some children like to express their ideas in poetry. Encourage them to do so. A poem does not need to rhyme. Some forms of poetry, like a cinquain, use line length rather than rhyme to make the poetic effect.

Writing activities also help a child to enjoy the thrill and self-confidence which comes when he has created something on his own. When a child must put his ideas into writing, he is helped to organize his thoughts. Even children who cannot yet write, or who find writing difficult, can participate in creative writing by dictating their thoughts to a leader who will write or tape them.

It is important to remember that children do not write out of a vacuum; they need careful preparation for the activity. This is especially true of song or poem writing. Before asking a child to attempt these, be sure he has had a wealth of other experiences from which to draw. For example, to lead pupils to write a poem about God's care, a teacher could do some or all of these things: (1) tell a Bible story, such as Elijah and the ravens; (2) discuss the story and its meaning, making clear the ways God cared for Elijah; (3) let pupils make a list of some evidences of God's care in their lives; and (4) play songs which emphasize God's care. After this, the teacher may lead the children to combine their thoughts about God's care into a poem.

It is also important to remember that because writing is very laborious, some children do not like writing activities. For these children, offer another activity choice—perhaps drawing, or even tape recording his thoughts.

Bible Learning Through Books and Research

The world pictured in the Bible is very different from the world in which today's boys and girls live. How can we help children better understand life in Bible days, relate this to our lives now, or gain other helpful information? One good way is through research activities.

The word *research* sounds very sophisticated, but it simply means "to study and find information." There are many different research activities suitable for children. Pupils may (1) view a filmstrip; (2) listen to a tape recording or record; (3) read a story or short article; (4) interview another person; or (5) take a field trip.

Some children are avid readers. For them, provide books of all sorts—Bible story books, books about Bible life and customs, and books of modern-day stories. With the book provide an activity which will help the child look for particular information and record what he learns. For example, with a Bible story provide cutout shapes of something featured in the story. On each shape write a question and leave room for the pupil to record his answer. If you cover the question card with clear Con-Tact paper or any brand of self-adhesive clear plastic, it can be used over and over again.

Another fun way for pupils to record their research findings is on a "Thinkback Board." This is simply a light-colored piece of poster board on which you have drawn lines. The finished board is glued to cardboard and covered with Con-Tact paper. Pupils can write on the board with a crayon or grease pencil, then erase it with facial tissue or paper towels.

Research activities may be done as a project in themselves or as part of other learning activities. A group who wants to make a frieze on the life of David might gain the facts they need in these ways: (1) read books; (2) view a filmstrip; or (3) listen to a story record. Pupils writing a chart report on "Ways God Helps Christians Today" could interview members of the church.

When pupils have completed their research, give them opportunities to share their new information with others, either as part of another learning activity or as a special report. In this way the research done by one adds to the learning of all.

Bible Learning Through Oral Communication

Most children love to talk. Because of this, they respond well to all sorts of discussion activities. Some of these methods have rather sophisticated names—but all are basically ways of guiding children to share their ideas.

Most children are not hesitant to talk if the class atmosphere is warm, accepting, and open. Even if they are slow to contribute ideas at first, do not be discouraged. Give the pupils time to really think before you give the answer or use another question to stimulate conversation.

Here are a few discussion methods which work well.

Brainstorming. This is a process of rapidly giving as many different ideas as possible, all related to a particular problem. It is an especially effective way to encourage pupils to think creatively, because no idea—however improbable it seems—is judged until all ideas have been given. This form of discussion stimulates ideas because pupils can often come up with variations of ideas that have already been presented. Only after all ideas are given are any evaluated and further refined.

Buzz Session. For this activity, pupils are divided into small groups. Each group is then given a question or problem to discuss and share later with the other groups. A good way to encourage discussion is to give pupils an open-ended story. They decide what "should be done" in that situation.

One teacher, fearing too much noise in the class, used an interesting approach to introduce buzz sessions. She compared the sounds pupils would make to the quiet buzz-buzz of a bee. When the noise level rose too high, it took only a gentle reminder to get things quieter again.

Older children can buzz independently; younger boys and girls will need a teacher or helper in their group to keep things going and to record group decisions.

Listening Teams. This method is especially good to use when pupils are hearing a Bible story or a special speaker. Divide the group into smaller groups and assign each one something specific to listen for. Doing this helps pupils to focus their attention on what is being said.

Question and Answer. There is a real art to asking questions which stimulate discussion and not just yes or no answers. Children are clever. It doesn't usually take them long to figure out, by the way a teacher asks a question, what the "right" answer should be. To avoid this problem, follow these guidelines for asking questions.

1. Avoid questions which can be answered simply with yes or no. Instead of asking, "Did Joseph trust God?" use the question, "What were ways that Joseph showed he trusted God?"

2. Use questions which call for pupils' opinions—"How do you think you would have felt if . . . ?" A question like this not only brings in opinions, but also differing opinions. This helps to spark the discussion even further. Words and phrases like "How?" "What do you think?" and "Why?" really help to elicit pupils' ideas.

3. Avoid suggesting the "right" answer when you ask a , question. Instead of "We should never tell lies, should we?" ask, "Why is it wrong to tell lies?"

4. Don't be too quick to reject an idea that may seem wrong. Ask a few more questions, such as "Tell me a little more about that"; or "What about such and such?" If a pupil is obviously off base, say, "That is one idea. Does anyone have another?" This acknowledges the child's contribution and avoids directly criticizing him for being wrong.

Children often discuss better if you use a visual aid or something else concrete to which they can react. For example, in one lesson the subject for discussion was "Courage." To help pupils focus their attention, the teacher wrote sentences, each one beginning with a different letter from the word *courage:* "*C*ome on, are you chicken?" and "*O*nly sissies read the Bible." As pupils read the sentences, they were helped to think of and discuss times when they had faced similar situations.

The teacher who is not too quick to superimpose his ideas on the pupils will find discussion activities a real clue to their thoughts, ideas, and growth in learning. As pupils share with each other, their understanding of other points of view also widens. This is an important step in growth which leads to Christian maturity.

Bible Learning Through Bible Games

"Let's play a game!" These magic words almost instantly bring a sparkle of delight into the eyes of boys and girls. Why? Because children love to play games. Listen to them for a short while, and sooner or later you'll hear the words "Let's play house . . . jacks . . . baseball . . . Scrabble."

Children enjoy playing games but they also learn from them. In addition, when boys and girls know that they will soon be playing a game which requires them to know certain information, they work harder at learning what is required. Sometimes a game is just the right thing to help bring new material to life. But not just any game is suitable for use in the church. Our teaching time is limited and precious. We must use it to best advantage in teaching God's Word to children. Therefore, in order to be a valid teaching tool at church, a Bible game must do one or more of these things.

1. Teach Bible facts and truths.
2. Review Bible facts and truths.
3. Develop skills in using the Bible and applying Bible truths to life.
4. Introduce a new unit.
5. Lead into Bible study.
6. Aid in Bible memorization and understanding.

There are many different game techniques which lend excitement to Bible learning. But it is the questions used which determine the effectiveness of the game. The questions must help to meet one of the six goals listed above. However, they can be stated in a variety of ways: true-false, multiple choice, missing words, riddles, matching, or paraphrase.

One of your best sources of Bible games is the teaching resource packets which correlate with Sunday school lesson materials. There is usually at least one game in each packet. Most of these can be used over and over again if you will just write new questions to cover the material you are currently studying. For instructions in making and using a variety of reusable games, order the book *Let's Teach with Bible Games,* by Donna Fillmore. It is available from the Nazarene Publishing House.

Bible games are excellent both for small group and for total class use. They are great to use during presession and/or in learning centers. Once they understand the game rules, older children can usually operate most Bible games by themselves. This frees the teacher to guide other pupils in other simultaneous learning experiences.

Class discipline needs to be watched with care during a game activity. Because games are exciting, it is easy for pupils to become rowdy—perhaps shouting out answers or arguing over game rules. Do not allow this to happen. Clearly give the behavior guidelines you expect as the game is played. If pupils do not comply, after a warning or two, simply stop the game for that time. After an experience or two of this kind, most children will heed your instructions.

Bible Learning Through Music Activities

Music is one of the most meaningful ways to teach new ideas to children. Not only do children learn faster, but they remember longer. For example, many adults who were taught the chorus naming the 12 apostles can still sing it today—and thus recall the apostles as well. Not only that, but a great many Christian concepts which people possess have been impressed on their minds and hearts through music.

Unfortunately, because music is so closely associated with performance, many people are afraid to use it. Unless they sing or play unusually well, they avoid guiding boys and girls in musical activities.

The fact is, however, that even the teacher who cannot carry a tune in a bucket can provide meaningful music experiences for children. Here are just a few of these.

Listening Activities. During presession or worship time, provide records or tapes for pupils to enjoy. To guide their listening, give the child an activity to do related to the song. For example, write the name of a song on a sheet of paper and print questions which can be answered from the song words. Ask the pupil to answer the questions when he has finished listening. Or give an assignment such as this: "Listen to 'He Cares for Me.' Draw a picture of one thing in your life that shows how God cares for you."

Musical Instruments. Children enjoy rhythm instruments and can use them effectively to "orchestrate" music. This simply means that the child makes up a rhythm accompaniment to the song. As children listen to music, help them to pick out the beat of the song—1-2-3, or 1-2-3-4. Then, help them to see the various things they can do with the instruments to emphasize the song rhythm in an interesting way. The different sounds that the instruments make form a nice accompaniment to the music.

One Christmas, a teacher brought a recording of "The Little Drummer Boy" to his class. He helped the pupils discover some interesting features about the song—for example, the repeated refrain "pah-rum-pah-pah-pum." Several children imitated this sound with rhythm sticks. Others used triangles to tap out a steady 1-2-3-4 throughout the song, giving the effect of chimes. The result was a beautiful musical creation.

Children can also learn to use other instruments such as tone blocks, a ChromAharP, or a zither.

Illustrating Songs. This is another excellent activity which helps children focus on the meanings of song words. Some songs have concrete objects to picture. "Gifts from Our Father" is a good example of this. The song names corn, wheat, the sun, apples, and a variety of other such things. Children can also illustrate song thoughts like this:

> *Friends of Jesus must be loving,*
> *Kind in all we do and say;*
> *Showing love and gladly sharing*
> *In our work and in our play.*[2]

Although in this song they will not illustrate individual words, they can draw pictures to clarify concepts such as being kind, sharing, working, and playing.

Illustrating a song has two values: first, it is an excellent learning activity to teach the meaning of the song; second, when the illustrations are finished, the resulting book or chart can be used when the children sing.

Writing Songs. It won't be Handel's *Messiah,* but children can (1) write new words to existing tunes; or (2) write new words and new tunes. Writing songs gives children an opportunity to express their feelings about something they have learned. Follow the same general procedures you would for writing a poem or story. In addition, help the children work their ideas into a song tune, or create a tune to fit the words they have written.

These are only a few ways you can use music to enhance children's learning experiences. There are many more. For a thorough and complete discussion of the values of music, ways music may be used, and methods for teaching new songs, be sure to read *The Ministry of Music with Children,* by Ethel Bailey. This book is interesting to read and has a wealth of practical, workable ideas.

What About Bible Memorization?

Although Bible memorization is not a "method" in the same sense as the other techniques we have discussed, it is an important Bible learning activity for children.

Why should children memorize Bible verses? Because children have spiritual needs just as adults do—and God's Word will help them meet those needs. A store of Bible verses which he knows "by heart" is always available when the child needs spiritual strength and guidance. Here are guidelines for making memorization effective.

Bible memorization involves more than just the ability to parrot words. In addition to being able to quote the words correctly, the child needs to understand the meaning of what he is memorizing. He also needs to be able to relate what he has learned to his own life.

Helping the child to understand what a Bible verse means is more important than just teaching the words. No matter how many verses he can quote—even entire chapters—the child is not helped if he does not know what those verses mean. If he does not understand it, he cannot use a Bible verse to help him solve a problem or answer a question.

Helping a child to understand what a Bible verse means is not always as easy as it might seem. The limited experience of the child sometimes leads to strange interpretations of God's Word. And the fact that there is so much symbolism in the Bible often complicates the teaching process, because children take symbolic words literally. Some of this misunderstanding can be overcome when we encourage the child to use the Bible verses he knows. When those verses contain symbolic words, give him opportunity to tell what those words mean. He will enjoy sharing his knowledge—and the teacher can check his understanding of what he has memorized.

Repetition is a most important factor in memorization. This is more than just rote repeating of the words. Repetition also occurs when the children have opportunities to see the material frequently, to speak the words, to hear the words spoken, and to use the material in a meaningful way.

Use variety as you teach Bible verses to children. Your Sunday school (or other) curriculum materials contain games, matching exercises, and other activities to help the child learn God's Word. Ideas may also be given for drawing an illustration, writing a story, or composing a song—all good ways to help the child learn Bible verses. One of the most effective teaching methods is to use the verses in ordinary conversation as you talk with children about events and experiences.

When God's Word is made meaningful to the child—when he sees for himself that the Bible verses he learns help him in daily living—he is much more likely to learn. And then he is learning more than Bible words; he is also learning Bible truth.

In this discussion of methods, we have been able to give only a glimpse of the many ways and means you can use to teach boys and girls. Hopefully, this discussion has served to whet your appetite to learn more. If so, you have two major sources of information—the curriculum materials for the various age-level ministries, and additional resource books on teaching methods. Curriculum materials provide specific guidance for using a method in a given situation. Books from the bibliography of this text will broaden your general knowledge of effective ways to teach children. It has been wisely said that "a little learning is a dangerous thing." As a leader of children's leaders, you will want to set the example for diligent effort in learning how best to make the Bible come alive for boys and girls.

REFERENCE NOTES

1. Elsiebeth McDaniel and Lawrence O. Richards, *You and Children* (Chicago: Moody Press, 1973), p. 88.

2. "When We Are Friends of Jesus," *Children's Praises,* enl. ed., comp. Joy Latham (Kansas City: Lillenas Publishing Co., 1964), p. 135.

And all thy children shall be taught
of the Lord; and great shall be the
peace of thy children.

Isa. 54:13, KJV

6

A Kaleidoscope of Children's Ministries

The Eighteenth General Assembly in 1972 ordered a commission to study the programs, organization, and structure of the Church of the Nazarene at the local, district, and general levels. The commission was to make recommendations to eliminate overlap and/or duplication of age-group programming, promotion, and materials. It was also asked to recommend the type of organizational structure needed to more effectively carry out the mission of the church.

At the Nineteenth General Assembly in 1976, the commission presented its report and referred it to the General Board for implementation. This action was to have far-reaching implications for the children and children's workers in the Church of the Nazarene. The commission recommended that the Departments of Church Schools and Youth be replaced by a Division of Christian Life which would include three departments —the Department of Children's Ministries (birth through 11 years), the Department of Youth Ministries (12-23 including college and singles), and the Department of Adult Ministries (24 years and older, or married). The commission felt this plan would eliminate the overlap of responsibility and the duplication of programs which had existed when more than one department had the responsibility of programming for the same age-groups.

The new Division of Christian Life is designed to accomplish the mission of the church at the local level through the support of the district and general church organizations. Children's ministries in the local church are served by the programs, materials, and promotion developed at the general and district levels.

The duties of the General Department of Children's Ministries are outlined in the 1976 Church of the Nazarene *Manual* (paragraphs 340.1 through 340.7) as follows:

1. To provide program and materials to minister to the needs of children from birth through 11 years and in harmony with the Word of God and the doctrines and polity of the Church of the Nazarene and subject to the General Board and Board of General Superintendents.

2. To promote the organization and work of children's Sunday schools, children's church, summer ministries, including vacation Bible schools, Caravans, camps, Bible clubs, Bible quizzing, missionary education (in cooperation with NWMS), and other Christian education and evangelism activities as assigned by the General Assembly or the General Board.

3. To prepare for publication materials and guidance for children's ministries in the local church and on the districts that are biblically, doctrinally, and theologically according to Nazarene interpretation and in line with the best educational principles. Curriculum materials will be coordinated with the Departments of Youth Ministries and Adult Ministries through the Coordinating Council to provide continuous learning experiences from childhood through adulthood. Evangelism and Christian nurture are to permeate these materials and guidance.

4. To provide general, regional, and district children's leadership training conferences, seminars, and workshops; training for local and district children's workers in cooperation with the Christian Service Training Agency; and resource people for equipping local district leaders, training texts, resources, and periodicals as needed to meet the leadership needs and equip these leaders for children's ministry.

5. To plan and provide for a general convention coordinated with the Departments of Youth Ministries and Adult Ministries to be constituted with representatives elected from the district in accordance with the bylaws of the Sunday school.

6. To meet annually as a Children's Curriculum and Program Committee, reviewing carefully the programs and curriculum materials, modifying as seems desirable, and giving final approval to all programs and materials provided for in children's ministries. Publication plans shall be in harmony with the editorial policy agreed upon by the Children's Ministries department, the Coordinating Council, and the Department of Publication.

7. To elect an editorial director to be a member of the Coordinating Council from nominations by the executive

director with the approval of the executive coordinator and the Board of General Superintendents.

In summary, the new Department of Children's Ministries has been given the task of providing leadership and resources for a coordinated total ministry to children. The function of the department is to help both districts and local churches meet the basic needs of children in the area of Christian education. These needs can be grouped into three categories of ministry: Bible knowledge and life application; worship; and fellowship.

To help churches and districts meet children's needs in these three areas, the Department of Children's Ministries provides a variety of programs and activities. Like the bits of colored glass in a kaleidoscope, these are many and varied— but each has its distinctive characteristics. These may be combined and implemented in different ways by different churches, but all go together to form a pattern of total ministry to meet the needs of children.

Sunday school, Sunday evening lessons and training activities, Bible quizzing, mission education, and vacation Bible school generally provide opportunities for Bible learning and life application. Children's church seeks to fill the need for worship. And the Nazarene Caravan program, camping, recreation, and other activities give children opportunities to fellowship together. Most of the ministries help to meet more than one of the needs of children; but each one has a particular major emphasis.

To provide a total ministry to children, a church or district must be aware of their needs and determine whether they are being met in the programs currently being offered. If some needs are not being met, plans should be made to do so through a new ministry, as soon as resources and leadership personnel are available. However, emphasis should always be on meeting needs of children, not on implementing programs just because they are available.

The chapters to follow describe each of the ministries provided by the Department of Children's Ministries. To achieve a balanced program for children, ministries should be provided on Sunday, through the week, and annually. You will also want to consider the "special ministries" which do not fall into Sunday, weekday, or annual time slots, but which are an important part of a total ministry to children.

*Let our children partake of the
training that is in Christ.*
CLEMENT OF ROME

7

Sunday Ministries

I. SUNDAY SCHOOL

Sunday school. What do you think of when you hear those two words? What memories are brought to mind?

I remember:

—the first scripture verse I ever memorized—"And whoso shall receive one such little child in my name receiveth me" (Matt. 18:5, KJV).

—winning a picture of Jesus for bringing the most boys and girls to Sunday school

—my first Bible

—Christmas programs

—Mrs. Conover telling me that Jesus loved me

—the reds against the blues in the Sunday school contest

—winning a plaque for guessing the number of beans in a jar at the Sunday school picnic

—the three-legged race at the same picnic

The Nature and Purpose of the Sunday School

What is Sunday school? It is Bible study, friendship, and fellowship. A well-developed Sunday school program is the essential foundation of any total ministry to children. It is central and primary to the work of the church because it is the major avenue for Christian education. Sunday school is the response of the church to the Great Commission's command to teach (cf. Matt. 28:19-20).

The purpose of the Sunday school is threefold: (1) to teach the Word of God effectively until pupils are saved, sanctified wholly, and maturing in Christian experience; (2) to help Christians grow spiritually by involving them in a reaching, teaching, and soul-winning ministry; and (3) to locate and visit un-churched people until they become enrolled and regular in attendance.

Although many different things take place during the Sunday morning hour—Bible study, worship, and fellowship—it is vital to remember that the distinctive focus of Sunday school is Bible study. It is this that makes Sunday school Sunday school and not something else.

Curriculum for Bible Study

To help local churches provide Bible study appropriate for all pupils, the Church of the Nazarene has prepared curriculum materials for children of all ages—nursery, kindergarten, primary, middler, and junior. Each age-level curriculum is planned specifically to help the child of that age study the Bible at his level of understanding and ability.

Nazarene Sunday school materials for children are part of a total curriculum plan. This plan is based on three important ideas which have helped to shape the curriculum. These are: (1) facts become important when they fit together to form concepts; (2) ideas worth knowing in adulthood need to be presented, reinforced, and expanded upon at various stages of the learner's development; and (3) real learning results in a changed life. Let us take a closer look at each of these guiding principles.

Christian educators have discovered that in order for Bible learning to be meaningful, the facts, stories, and scriptures which the pupil encounters in individual lessons must be related to larger concepts. For example, pupils must be able to relate the events of Jesus' life and ministry to the larger concept of understanding God's plan for the world and for a particular human life.

To achieve this goal, Nazarene curriculum is organized around 12 quarterly themes or important concepts pupils should know. In units and individual lessons, these themes are broken down into smaller concept units which are on the understanding level of the pupil. Take a look at these on the chart on pp. 108-9.

The second important idea underlying Nazarene curriculum is that what is really worth knowing as an adult can be taught to pupils of any age, when presented on their level of understanding; and these concepts should be reinforced and expanded upon at periodic intervals. For example, is it important for adults to understand how to make decisions which are based on the Christian ethic? If so, this idea—with the related ideas of how to make decisions, how to evaluate decisions, and standards for making Christian decisions—needs to be introduced to young children. Even a primary child is involved in decision making; he can, and should, learn how to make Christian decisions on a primary level.

But what happens when the learner becomes a middler or a junior? Because he is older, the number and type of decisions he makes is increasing. He needs to look at the decision-making process again and explore additional ways to make Christian decisions. This same procedure should be repeated as the child matures.

Our curriculum is built in such a way that nursery and kindergarten children repeat the same cycle of themes every two years. Primary, middler, and junior children repeat the quarterly themes every three years. Thus, all the important concepts are repeated throughout the life of the learner from grades 1 through 12.

This does not mean that the learner reviews the same lessons every three years. He studies the same basic idea, but in a different way and on a more mature level. For example, in the second quarter of the first year of the curriculum cycle all pupils, first grade through senior high, deal with the concept of basic beliefs. But each age-group treats this concept on a level which the pupils can understand and which applies to their daily living. This planned repetition is known as a "spiral" curriculum.

Not only is Nazarene curriculum a "spiral" curriculum, but it is also a "stacked" curriculum. The repetition of ideas and concepts is planned carefully so the learner does not study

Correlated Teaching

Adult	Enduring Word Series					

	Year 1				Year 2	
	SON* QUARTER	DJF QUARTER	MAM QUARTER	JJA QUARTER	SON QUARTER	DJF QUARTER
Quarterly Themes	The Story of the Old Testament People	Basic Beliefs	Discipleship: Interpersonal Relations	The Church	The Message of the Bible	Men of God
Senior High	The Universe—God's Creation Life Experiences from Old Testament Characters	What Can I Believe?	Getting Along with Myself Getting Along with Others	The Church of Jesus the Christ Christ's Coming— When and How?	Study in Galatians The Unfolding Plan of Redemption	The Prophets Came to Main Street
Junior High	What We Believe About the Bible Exploring the Old Testament	Basic Beliefs About God Ten Commandments for Teens	Christ's Call to Discipleship (Salvation) Living with Others	How the Church Began My Place in the Church The Church Goes Abroad	When God Speaks The Message of the Bible	Decisions for Destiny The Book of Jonah
Junior	A Look at My Bible Bits of Biography	What I Believe Keeping the Commandments Today	Getting Along Together Really Living Christians in Hard Places	My Church in History What My Church Believes My Church in Mission	God's Plan for His People	Adventures with God
Middler	Learning About My Bible Learning to Walk with God Joseph Lives for God	Moses, God's Man for a Big Job Rules for Right Living	Jesus Shared God's Love We Share God's Love	Learning About the Church My Place in the Church My Church Around the World	How We Got Our Bible The Message of the Bible	The Story of Christmas Serving God at All Times
Primary	Abraham and His Family Follow God The Bible, God's Wonderful Book	Because Jesus Came God's Rules for Right Living What Jesus Taught About God	Bible Friends of Jesus Workers Together with God	Our Church Good News for All the World	Moses, a Chosen Leader The Wonderful Story of God's Love Giving Thanks for God's Steadfast Love	God's Gift at Christmas Adventurers with God
Kindergarten	2-year cycle					
Nursery	2-year cycle for twos and threes					

Chart

		Year 3			
MAM QUARTER	**JJA QUARTER**	**SON QUARTER**	**DJF QUARTER**	**MAM QUARTER**	**JJA QUARTER**
Discipleship: Personal Commitment	Decision-making as Christians	The Living God	The Life of Jesus	The Acts of the Apostles	Discipleship: Relationship to the World
Life at Its Best Life Put to the Test	The Choice Is Yours Book Study of James	Can We Trust the Bible? The Living God	Book Study of John	Book Study of John Doctrines, Problems, and Practices of the Early Church	Proverbs
What It Means to Be a Christian Paul's Thank-you Letter	Lessons in Living	The Bible, God's Record The Living God	The Book of Luke	The Saviour for Me Christians in Action	Christians in Action Guidelines for Today
In the Days of Kings and Prophets (Part I) Seeking and Finding a Savior In the Days of Kings and Prophets (Part II)	God's People Punished and Restored Making Right Choices	The Living God Jesus Answers My Questions	The Life of Christ	Jesus Provides Salvation The Beginning of the Christian Church	The Church Grows Our Church at Work Around the World We Work with God
Jesus Makes a Difference First Steps for New Christians	Courage to Live for God Learning to Make Right Choices Special Choices Christians Must Make	We Learn About God from His World Learning About God from the Bible Loving and Worshiping God	Praising God for Jesus Jesus, the Son of God	Jesus, Our Savior Messengers for God	Guidelines for Christian Living Sharing the Gospel in India Using My Treasures for God
Living as Friends of Jesus Friends of Jesus Carry On His Work	Making Right Choices Learning to Pray and Praise	What God Is Like Songs of Praise to God	The Story of Jesus	The Story of Jesus Stories of the Early Church	Learning and Growing as God Planned Serving God Where You Are

Toddler — **NEW** 1-year cycle for toddlers

*SON—September, October, November

them in a hit-or-miss fashion. Notice that all pupils, primary through senior high, study the same topic areas in the same quarter. Because of this, when a child is promoted from one age-group to another, he will not have lessons which he has just studied.

Another important fact to notice is that although curriculum for primaries, middlers, and juniors is planned on a three-year-cycle (that is, every three years a pupil again studies the same concept ideas he encountered three years before), the pupils are grouped on the basis of two-year grading. Because of this, a pupil studies only two-thirds of the complete lesson cycle at any given age level. The chart below illustrates how this works.

	Year 1			Year 2			Year 3			Year 1			Year 2			Year 3		
Qtr.	1	2	3	4	5	6	7	8	9	10	11	12	1	2	3	4	5	6	7	8	9	10	11	12
J																	X	X	X	X	X	X	X	X
M										X	X	X	X	X	X	X	X Promoted to Junior							
P	X	X	X	X	X	X	X	X Promoted to Middler																

If a learner enters the curriculum plan as a primary, at the beginning of the cycle, he studies the first and second years of the cycle as a primary. When he is promoted to the Middler Department, he gets at that level the third year of the cycle and repeats the first year as well. As a junior, he finishes with the second and third years of the cycle again.

The third principle underlying Nazarene curriculum is that real learning results in a changed life. It is not enough to know Bible facts or even to understand Christian principles. In order for learning to be complete, the pupil must reflect his understandings in changed attitudes and behavior. In this area, the teacher must rely upon the Holy Spirit's working in the life of the pupil. Only God's Spirit can bring these results—and even the Holy Spirit must have the cooperation of the pupil's free will.

Good Bible teaching, however, is a prime factor in this

change. Without growth in knowledge, there is less likely to be
life change. The task of the Sunday school teacher is illustrated
on this chart.

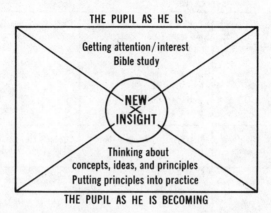

THE PUPIL AS HE IS

Getting attention/interest
Bible study

NEW
INSIGHT

Thinking about
concepts, ideas, and principles
Putting principles into practice

THE PUPIL AS HE IS BECOMING

Pupils come to Sunday school with a variety of needs,
interests, and even hindrances to learning. The teacher must
somehow capture the pupil's attention and focus it on the topic
for the day. When interest has been captured, pupils then go on
to study the Bible and see what God's Word says about the
idea under consideration. From the Bible study, pupils should
be helped to think about the implications and principles shown
in God's Word. They must ask, "What does this mean? What
does it mean in my life? In the lives of others?" And finally,
a good Sunday school lesson helps pupils explore ways to put
into practice the things they have discovered in class.

The part of the chart labeled "New Insight" is the part of
learning which the Sunday school teacher cannot dictate. We
cannot know when an idea or principle will really grab a pupil
and cause him to change in his attitude or behavior. Nor can
we make him do things differently from what he has done
before. But teachers can (1) make learning as interesting as
possible, so pupils will be more motivated to learn and change;
(2) involve pupils in every part of the lesson; and (3) pray
faithfully that the pupil will respond to the working of the
Holy Spirit. Nazarene curriculum materials are designed to give
the teacher the guidance he needs to achieve the goal of changed
lives.

Resources for Sunday School

For These Children	USE THESE MATERIALS	
	Child	Teacher
CRADLE ROLL—from birth until fourth birthday, and not enrolled in Sunday school	1. **First Steps Toward God**—a two-year packet of guidance for parents and pieces for the child 2. **Toddler Bible Story Cards**—for the one-year-old 3. **Nursery Bible Stories**—for two- and three-year-olds	Cradle Roll visitor takes material into the home.
NURSERY CRIB—birth until first birthday	**First Steps Toward God**—to be taken into the home	Sunday school worker takes material into the home.
NURSERY I—one-year-olds	**Toddler Bible Story Cards**	1. **Toddler Teacher** 2. **Toddler Teaching Resources** 3. **Toddler Bible Story Cards**
SUNDAY SCHOOL NURSERY CLASS—two- and three-year-olds	1. **Nursery Bible Stories** 2. **Nursery Activities** 3. **Listen** (story paper)	1. **Nursery Teacher** 2. **Nursery Teaching Resources** 3. **Nursery Bible Stories** 4. **Nursery Activities** 5. **Listen** (story paper)
KINDERGARTEN—four- and five-year-olds (and six-year-olds not yet in grade one)	1. **Kindergarten Bible Stories** 2. **Kindergarten Activities** 3. **Listen** (story paper)	1. **Kindergarten Teacher** 2. **Kindergarten Teaching Resources** 3. **Kindergarten Bible Stories** 4. **Kindergarten Activities** 5. **Listen** (story paper)
PRIMARY—grades one and two	1. **Primary Bible Stories** 2. **Primary Activities** 3. **Wonder Time** (story paper)	1. **Primary Teacher** 2. **Primary Teaching Resources** 3. **Primary Bible Stories** 4. **Primary Activities** 5. **Wonder Time** (story paper)
MIDDLER—grades three and four	1. **Bible Explorers** 2. **Discoveries** (story paper)	1. **Middler Teacher** 2. **Middler Teaching Resources** 3. **Bible Explorers** 4. **Discoveries** (story paper)
JUNIOR—grades five and six	1. **Junior Adventures with the Bible** 2. **Discoveries** (story paper)	1. **Junior Teacher** 2. **Junior Teaching Resources** 3. **Junior Adventures with the Bible** 4. **Discoveries** (story paper)

Organization of the Sunday School

In order for children to receive the benefit of age-level Bible study, the Sunday school needs to be organized by grades and departments. This type of structure makes possible (1) the best use of age-level curriculum materials; and (2) effective administration of the Sunday school. Administration simply means getting things done by other people. A Sunday school that is correctly graded and departmentalized is a school where things get done more easily and more effectively. For example, when a school is large enough to have two classes of the same age-group, it is ready for supervision. The best teacher can be made responsible for guiding and helping a less-experienced teacher. When the school has three classes of the same age-group, and has space for those pupils to meet as a department, the supervisor should be relieved of classroom duty. He then has more time to observe and help the other teachers. The result will be better Bible teaching for the pupils, and a more satisfying experience for the teachers.

Departmentalization also makes greater Sunday school growth possible. Studies of growing denominations have shown that each time new classes or departments are added to a school, growth is encouraged. In addition, a departmentalized school gives more people an opportunity to become actively involved in the Christian education of children.

Even the smallest Sunday school should divide children into at least two broad groups; preschool children (birth through age five), and elementary children (grades one through six). As the Sunday school grows, these age-groups should be further divided.

The chart on page 114 shows the most effective ways to grade and departmentalize pupils in churches of all sizes. When a class or department begins to approach optimum size, it is time to divide the group. Even though it may not be possible to have separate department worship services, it is important to establish department organization. The work of each age-group becomes more effective when a supervisor is appointed and made responsible for planning and promoting the interests of the pupils and classes in that group. Information about appropriate rooms, learning environment, and teaching methods for children is given in the two chapters on ministering to preschoolers and elementary children.

Division Chart for Departmentalizing a Nazarene Sunday School

Approximate Attendance	Department Rooms		DEPARTMENTS						
25	1	Ages Pupils Classes	Children 2-11 10 2						
50	2	Ages Pupils Classes*	Children 2-11 19 4						
75	3	Ages Pupils Classes*	Preschool 0-5 12 3 groups			Children 6-11 21 3			
100	4	Ages Pupils Classes**	Preschool 0-5 16 4 groups			Children 6-11 28 4			
150	6	Ages Pupils Classes**	Nursery 0-3 12 3 groups	Kindergarten 4-5 12		Primary 6-7 14 2	Middler 8-9 14 2	Junior 10-11 14 2	
200	7	Ages Pupils Classes	Nursery 0-3 16 3 groups	Kindergarten 4-5 16 3 groups		Primary 6-7 18 3	Middler 8-9 18 3	Junior 10-11 20 3	
300	9	Ages Pupils Classes	Crib & Toddler Nursery 0-1 9 2	Nursery for Twos 2 8 2	Nursery for Threes 3 8 2	Kindergarten 4 | 5 12 | 12 3 | 3	Primary 6-7 27 4	Middler 8-9 27 4	Junior 10-11 27 4
400	13	Ages Pupils Classes	Crib & Toddler Nursery 0-1 10 2	Nursery for Twos 2 10 2	Nursery for Threes 3 12 3	Kindergarten 4 | 5 16 | 16 3 | 3	Primary 6 | 7 18 | 18 3 | 3	Middler 8 | 9 18 | 18 3 | 3	Junior 10 | 11 18 | 18 3 | 3
500 and over			Schools 500 and over organize a department for each age or grade from nursery through junior.						

Departments

1. The boxes created by the light horizontal and heavy vertical lines indicate the number of rooms which should be available for department meeting areas.

Department Rooms

1. The number of department rooms recommended does not include a room for crib and one-year-old babies. A minimum of one room should always be provided for this group. The toddlers' room should be large enough to provide space needed for teaching activities with toddlers.

2. A large room for activity teaching should be used with nursery, kindergarten, and primary children. An open department room is approved housing for the middler, junior, and older when team teaching is used.

Preschool Area

*1. Preschool children should have a separate area even though another extra room is not available.

**2. Toddlers, two- and three-year-old children should be in separate groups even though another room is not available.

For Class and Department Expansion

	Maximum Enrollment Class	Maximum Attendance Class	Maximum Attendance Department
Nursery-Crib—0-12 mos.		4*	15
Nursery-Toddler—1 year		4*	15
Nursery—2 years	7*	4*	15
Nursery—3 years	8*	5*	20
Kindergarten	9	6	25
Primary	12	8	25
Middler	13	9	30
Junior	14	10	40

*For nursery and kindergarten children, this means the number of pupils per worker rather than a formal class. Procedure for toddlers through fives includes much small-group teaching in activity centers. See nursery booklets and kindergarten booklet for more specific guidance.

II. Children's Church

Do the following phrases produce mental images of any children's "worship" you have observed? Chairs askew; crumpled papers; tattered songbooks; chalkboard scribblings; outdated posters; children scuffling, poking; squeaking chairs; teachers chatting, thumbing through materials; pianist asking pages, shuffling music; leaders calling for order, raising voices; loud singing; mumbled prayers; ho-hum announcements; noisy offerings; Bible teaching; dismissal scramble![1] Is this really worship? If not, what does an experience like this, when labeled "worship," say to children about the importance and the practices of worship? As we think about these questions, it is essential to know what we mean when we speak of worship.

What Is Worship?

It is easy to talk about worship, but it is difficult to narrow the discussion down to a definition. Worship is appreciating God for who He is. It is the loving response of an individual's heart to a consciousness of God's presence. The entire experience of communion with God is worship. Ralph D. Heim, in

Leading a Church School, gives the following definition of worship:

"Worship is an activity that includes, when complete, six components: an outreach of the self toward God; a felt inreach of God toward the self; resultant communion; some thought about things of God and godliness; an emotional reaction to the same; and above all, some response in peace, purpose, or action."[2]

The Bible tells us to glorify God. "Ascribe to the Lord the glory due his name; bring an offering and come into his courts. Worship the Lord in the splendor of his holiness; tremble before him, all the earth" (Psalm 96:8-9). If we do not worship God, we are not obeying Him. It also follows that if we do not teach our children to worship, we are also disobeying God.

Children's church is a worship service designed especially for children. It uses concepts they can understand and relate to their lives, presented in a variety of methods to hold their interest. It is a service in which they can participate physically, mentally, and spiritually.

Children's church has four important goals:
1. To strengthen the children's relationship with God
2. To allow boys and girls to have a worship experience appropriate for their age
3. To prepare them for participation in adult worship when they are older
4. To train them for service to God and the church

Children's church is not another Sunday school session, nor is it a time of entertainment, busywork, or baby-sitting while parents attend the adult service. Although children do not spend the entire church time in worship, worship is the focal point of the session. All other activities should be planned around the worship theme and objectives, either to introduce or reinforce them.

What Happens in Children's Church?

The three major elements of a Sunday morning children's church are the transition time, worship time, and activity time. Activity time may be scheduled before or following the worship, but it should either prepare for or reinforce the worship emphasis.

Transition Time

The period between Sunday school and church, plus an additional 10 minutes or so, is called Transition Time. This gives the children an opportunity to "change gears" from the Sunday school hour to church time, and to take care of rest room needs. Also during this time, you may schedule activities such as these: refreshments, games, fellowship, learning new songs, and preparing bulletin boards. The atmosphere of transition time should be orderly but informal. The children need this opportunity to relax a bit before they proceed to the worship service.

Worship

Worship is the focal point and the most important part of children's church. The worship time usually includes five elements: scripture; music; prayer; offering; and a devotional feature. The order of the service should be varied to meet the needs of the pupils.

The scripture used needs to be appropriate for the age-group and the objective of the worship time. Hearing the Word can lead children to worship.

Grace McGavran, in *Learning How Children Worship,* discusses two ways that scriptures are misused in worship. Responsive reading which breaks up a scripture portion verse by verse may destroy the meaning and cause the child to focus on when to start and stop rather than on what is being read. The second misuse is asking children to read aloud passages which are too difficult for their reading ability. Reading mistakes produce self-consciousness and embarrassment, not worship. Children should be given time to prepare before being asked to read scripture aloud to the group.[3]

There are many ways that scriptures can be used creatively during the worship time. Posters, drama, slides, choral readings, overhead transparencies—all of these can be used to make the scriptures more meaningful to children.

Music is an important part of the worship time. It can set the tone for worship and give children a means of expressing how they feel. It can also strengthen a desire to serve God. Because of this, songs for the worship time need to be chosen carefully. Singing needs to be a true worship experience which helps a child meet God. Worship is not the time to use catchy choruses or action songs which cause children to become noisy and excited. Rather, songs should emphasize the attributes of God and tell how He works in our lives. Older middlers and juniors can learn and enjoy some of the lovely hymns of the church.

To guide your selection of songs for children's worship, ask yourself these questions:

1. Is the music within the child's range, easy to sing, and of good quality?
2. Is the length, vocabulary, and content suitable for the age-group?
3. Do the children understand what they are singing so they can worship, or are the words figurative and abstract?
4. Are the words scripturally and doctrinally correct?

Worship time is not the time to teach new songs. This should be done during transition or activity times. Then during the worship service, children can sing songs they know as an expression of love and praise to God.

Prayer is an essential part of worship. It is our opportunity to talk with God and express our feelings to Him. Children's church leaders should plan a specific time for prayer. However, they should also be open to the leading of the Holy Spirit to show them when the children are ready to turn to God.

Children should be helped to feel comfortable with prayer. Mary LeBar says that the best way to teach a child to pray aloud is to begin so early that he can't remember having to learn. However, because this has not been the experience of all children, she also suggests that we not call on a child to pray before the group without asking him ahead of time. In this way, we are sure of his willingness.[4]

One way to encourage children to grow in their willingness to pray is through prayer requests. Ask the children to share their concerns, and list these for all to see. Call on adults to pray, but ask children to volunteer to pray silently for specific items. As they become involved in each other's needs, their willingness to pray aloud often grows.

Children need to be taught that *the offering* is a personal act of commitment. Encouraging them to bring money which they have earned will help them begin to learn that sacrificial giving means giving something that is valuable. Children need to be told what the offering is for and how it will be used. They need to understand the "why" of giving.

The devotional feature is the message or lesson for children. Workers need to be aware of the needs and characteristics of the children in their group and present messages which will meet those needs.

Since worship involves the heart and feelings as well as the intellect, a variety of methods should be used to present the message. Devotionals can be dramatized, visualized, or projected. Stories, art, poetry, and puppets can be used, as long as they do not become so entertaining that a spirit of reverence is negated.

It is important to make sure that the message is one children can really understand and gain spiritual help from. Many so-called object talks for children are highly symbolic and convey ideas which only confuse boys and girls. The devotional message needs to contain concrete spiritual guidance which children can readily understand and apply to life.

Activity Time

The third major portion of children's church is the activity time. This portion of the session—which should be about 30 minutes long—includes appropriate activities to reinforce the message or to expand on the objective for the day. Activity time is not just a busywork time provided because children are tired of sitting. Nor should it be considered a "craft" period. Rather, it is a time when children engage in learning activities which relate to the Bible materials and life-related truths they encountered in worship. Suitable activities could include dramatizing the Bible story, Bible quizzing, scripture memorization, Bible games, creative art, creative writing, missionary projects, and crafts. The activities should be varied from Sunday to Sunday.

Personnel

Qualified leaders are so important that it is wiser to delay the organization of children's church than to begin with the wrong people. The director is elected by the Board of Christian Life, upon nomination by the pastor, chairman of the Board of Christian Life, and the director of children's ministries.

The number of leaders necessary will depend on the number of groups and the number of children in each group. The minimum personnel needed is a director and a pianist. Other helpers can be added as the group grows.

The responsibilities of the children's church director are listed below:

1. Is the children's church representative on the Children's Council.
2. Plans with the pastor and director of children's ministries for workers needed.
3. Sets the age limits for children's church.
4. Surveys facilities. Provides for adequate space far enough away from the sanctuary to eliminate the possibility of either adults or children disturbing each other's worship services.
5. Recommends through the Children's Council a plan for financing the program.
6. Recommends and orders all materials.
7. Sets goals and plans with the workers.
8. Works out schedules.
9. Publicizes the program.
10. Enlists prayer partners.
11. Leads the weekly children's church service, or supervises those who do.

Grouping and Grading

Children should be grouped for children's church as nearly as possible by the same departments and age-group divisions used in Sunday school. It is especially important to separate preschool and elementary-age children. Children's church for preschoolers is called "extended session." Although it contains the same basic elements as we have discussed in this chapter, it is less structured than children's church for elementary children. When preschool and elementary children are combined for worship, the result is an unsatisfactory experience for everyone.

Whenever possible, primaries, middlers, and juniors should also be divided for worship. However, some churches are not able to do this because of limited space or leadership, or because the number in each group would be too few for effective group worship. If it is impossible to have three separate groups, there are several alternatives:

1. Combine primary, middler, and junior groups, but insofar as possible provide separate activities and extra workers for guiding these activities. When this group reaches 40 in attendance, make a positive effort to divide into at least two groups to make possible a closer relationship between leader and child and to give more opportunity for interaction.
2. Combine ages 6 through 9 and send juniors (10-11-year-olds) to adult worship.
3. Have only a primary church for first and second graders. Send all middlers and juniors to adult church.

It is important to determine the age limits and to enforce them. It is a mistake to allow a nursery or kindergarten child to attend children's church simply because he has an older brother or sister there. It is also a mistake to allow older children to remain in the group when they are past the age limit, unless they are being trained as helpers in the younger group.

Transition from Children's Church to Adult Church

An important part of an effective children's church program is helping boys and girls make the transition to adult worship. This is especially important for middlers and juniors; but even primaries need to have experiences in the regular Sunday morning service. As a general guideline, plan for primaries to attend worship at least once a quarter or six months. Middlers should go even more often, and sixth grade juniors should be in worship at least once a month. It is usually better to plan to attend adult worship at the conclusion of a unit of study, rather than breaking its continuity.

There are many ways you can make adult worship a profitable experience for children. Prepare them for it by showing them a bulletin and explaining what to expect. Encourage older boys and girls to jot down at least one idea from the sermon to share with you the following week. The children will receive a more normal worship experience if they sit with their families, not as a special group. Those whose parents do not attend worship should be seated with a caring "adoptive" family.

When the children attend, encourage the pastor to make mention of the fact, and to include something in the worship service especially beamed toward children.

In Conclusion

The value of children's church has sometimes been questioned by concerned parents and pastors. In some instances, the criticisms have been valid. Because of poor teaching methods and/or inadequate supervision, children have sometimes been "taught" disrespect for God's house, rather than worship.

This need not be the case. A properly administered children's church effectively teaches children how to worship God on their own level. And it can be a prime means of preventing children from "turning off" or "tuning out" church because they are bored by an adult worship service that is meaningless to them.

Resources

Packets:	*Living to Please God* *God Has a Plan for Your Life* *Jesus Is Coming Again* *God Made You Special*
Program Books:	*52 Sundays of Worship for Children,* Books 1 and 2, by Emily Bushey Moore *Leading Children in Worship: 52 Complete Plans for Children's Church,* Robert D. Troutman, editor
Leader Helps:	*Planning Church Time for Children,* by Betty Robertson The *Exchange*
Songbooks:	*Songs of God and Me* *Sing!*

III. Evening Meetings

An additional opportunity for instruction and training is available in the 30-45-minute time period prior to Sunday evening service. There is no special curriculum for evening sessions; but the time can be used to schedule a variety of ministries and/or special activities. Many leaders use these options: lessons from *Kaleidoscope;* Bible quizzing; mission study; graded choirs; and special projects.

Reference Notes

1. Eleanor Hance, "Teaching Children to Worship and Pray" in Roy B. Zuck and Robert E. Clark, eds., *Childhood Education in the Church* (Chicago: Moody Press, 1975), p. 274.

2. Ralph D. Heim, *Leading a Church School,* cited by Eleanor Hance in Zuck and Clark, *Childhood Education in the Church,* p. 275.

3. Grace McGavran, *Learning How Children Worship* (St. Louis: The Bethany Press, 1964), pp. 55-56.

4. Mary E. LeBar, *Children Can Worship* (Wheaton, Ill.: Victor Books, 1971), p. 80.

*And Jesus increased in wisdom and
stature, and in favour with God
and man.*
Luke 2:52, KJV

Weekday Ministries

Laurie, age 10, was finding life particularly difficult at the moment. Her family had moved recently, first to a new state and town; and then, within just a year, she had been required to change schools because of a building and expansion program. Just when she had made friends, it seemed, she would be moved in one way or another. When she discovered that there were very few girls her age in the community or even in her Sunday school class, she began to feel increasingly lonely, isolated, and friendless.

Then Laurie discovered Caravan—and things began to change for the better. She loved the informal atmosphere and the wide range of interesting activities. Soon she developed a whole range of new skills and interests—sewing, camping, and even archery. But best of all, her loneliness and sense of isolation began to decline as she made new friends in her Pathfinder group. Her grateful parents later expressed to the Caravan guide how much the program had meant to their daughter. It had made a tremendous difference in the success of her adjustment to a new life in a new situation.

The Nazarene Caravan program is just one of a group of weekday ministries which are part of a total ministry to children.

What Are Weekday Ministries?

Weekday ministries are those ministries which are carried out some time between Sundays because their curriculum and learning activities are not geared for Sunday time periods. Some aspect of these weekday ministries closely resemble those of Sunday ministries; there are opportunities for Bible study, instruction in Christian living, and worship.

Activities such as these can easily be carried out on Sundays or integrated into other programs. But other aspects of the weekday programs are clearly different from Sunday kinds of experiences. This is particularly true of certain fellowship and achievement activities. Because of this, ministries such as Caravan, Quizzing, and often mission education are generally provided for children during the week. The unique emphases of these programs help to complete a total ministry to children.

I. THE NAZARENE CARAVAN PROGRAM

The Nazarene Caravan program is a weekday ministry designed to promote spiritual, mental, physical, and social development in children grades two through six. This development is accomplished through participation in a special curriculum of achievement work and advancement. Here are some of the special benefits of a Caravan program.

1. Caravan more than doubles the amount of time you have available to teach boys and girls. In addition to the weekly meetings which last at least an hour, sometimes more, successful completion of Caravan badges requires additional get-togethers of various sorts, such as camp-outs, service projects, and social happenings. Besides these things, the child must spend time at home working on requirements for his badges.

2. Caravan gives boys and girls opportunity for a broader and different kind of contact with Christians. Unlike Sunday school, the atmosphere of Caravan meetings and events is informal. One boy put it this way: "We get to wear our old clothes for doing grubby projects!" Children see Christian adults in times of relaxation—on a camp-out, or when working together on a craft activity. The wide variety of achievement areas also makes it possible to involve a greater number of church people in the program by allowing them to help on a

short-term basis. For example, one Caravan guide had a friend who was an excellent photographer. When the children were working on that badge, he invited his friend to come for a week or two and share his knowledge with them. The children benefited not only from learning about cameras, but also from having enjoyable interaction with yet another Christian man.

3. Caravan appeals to the club or gang spirit that is especially strong in boys and girls of this age. The children meet in groups of all boys or all girls, which is especially important to middlers and juniors. The program provides rituals and routines which give the child a sense of belonging to a special group.

4. Because Caravan is so appealing, it also increases the church's opportunities to reach out to children. Boys and girls who may show little interest in coming to Sunday school for Bible study are often attracted by the wide variety of interesting activities available through Caravan. Some churches use Caravan as their major means of outreach to children. Once a child is actively involved in the Caravan program, it is easier to encourage his attendance at Sunday school as well.

5. Caravan provides boys and girls additional opportunities to give service in the local church. It also provides a means through which more adults can become involved in ministry to children.

Objectives of the Caravan Ministry

The general objectives of the Caravan ministry are based on the four areas of development described in Luke 2:52: "And Jesus increased in wisdom and stature, and in favour with God and man" (KJV). Here is a summary of the objectives given in the *Manual* of the Church of the Nazarene.

To teach the doctrines of Christianity and the standards of Christian behavior as revealed in the Bible, especially as interpreted by the Articles of Faith in the *Manual* of the Church of the Nazarene.

Teaching doctrine is done throughout the entire Caravan program. The Brave/Maiden groups learn a catechism of 106 questions and answers about: God, Our Heavenly Father; The Bible; How Sin Began; Jesus, Our Savior; The Christian Life; The Church.

Trailblazer/Pathfinder groups learn two scriptures to support each of the 15 Articles of Faith in the *Manual.*

To seek the salvation of the unsaved and the entire sanctification of believers.

One of the special tasks of the Caravan is to make sure every boy and girl has ample opportunity to receive Jesus Christ as personal Savior and be led (as they are mature enough to do so) into a life of full commitment to the Holy Spirit.

To lay the foundation for, and foster the progressive and continuous development of, Christlike character, attitudes, and habits.

Character development involves the intertwining of moral principles with the whole personality of the individual. To achieve this goal, the Caravan program stresses spiritual growth activities, such as Bible reading, Bible memorization, and Sunday school participation. In addition, Braves and Maidens learn a Code of Honor, while Pathfinders and Trailblazers memorize a Code of Ethics. Both of these emphasize Christian moral behavior. The very nature of the activities in the Caravan program encourage growth in personal morality, such as fair play, sharing, and honest achievement.

To lead to the discovery of the Christian philosophy of life and the biblical interpretation of the universe.

A strong emphasis on outdoor activities helps boys and girls discover the wonders of God's handiwork in creation. This is just one of the ways in which children are helped to develop a Christian philosophy of life.

To help the home become more effective in teaching the Christian faith.

No other organization in the church asks for more cooperation from the home than Caravan. The family must work together to help the child advance in the program.

To influence strongly in favor of church membership and to train for service in the church.

In Caravan, the child is taught everything that is covered in the pastor's membership class. Caravan includes a study of the history of the Church of the Nazarene, its doctrines, the things the church does for him, and things he should do for the church.

To reach the largest number of people for Christ and the church.

Caravan is concerned with outreach. Guides are encouraged to find new members. Each Caravaner is asked to bring friends to share in this weekday activity.

Caravan Organization

On the local church level, children in the Nazarene Caravan program are organized into several different groups which are identified by a variety of titles. This organization is illustrated on the next page.

Notice that there are two large divisions of children in the program. All younger children (grades two and three) belong to a "tribe." All older children (grades four, five, and six) belong to a "camp."

Both the tribe and the camp are further divided into two groups each. Younger boys are known as Braves, younger girls as Maidens. Older boys are Trailblazers, and older girls Pathfinders. The leaders for these four groups are known as Brave Guides, Maiden Guides, Pathguides, and Trailguides.

Each individual group of Braves or Maidens is called a "wigwam." In a small church, both second and third grade boys may be combined into one Braves wigwam; second and third grade girls are combined into a Maiden wigwam. As the Caravan group grows, the wigwams may be further divided as shown, providing separate groups for second and third grade boys and girls.

Second and third grade boys and girls go by separate names, even when they are combined in the same wigwam.

Younger Girls—Indian Maidens
    Second grade girls—Silver Moon
    Third grade girls—Pocahontas

Younger Boys—Indian Braves
    Second grade boys—Hunters
    Third grade boys—Chiefs

Individual divisions of Trailblazers and Pathfinders are called "groups." In one group, you may have fourth, fifth, and sixth grade boys or girls. Or, you may divide into individual groups—one for each age level of boys and of girls.

Caravan Organization Chart

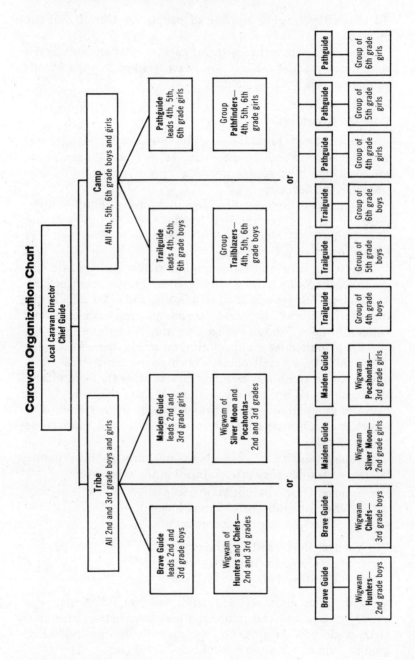

The local Caravan director, or Chief Guide, directs the entire local program and represents the ministry on the Children's Council. Even the smallest organization should have five leaders—a Chief Guide, plus one Brave Guide, one Maiden Guide, one Trailguide, and one Pathguide. Larger groups will have more than one guide in each division. Whenever possible, it is helpful to provide the guide with an assistant.

There are two prescribed curricula for younger children and one for older children. Boys and girls in the second grade each receive a book which they study, and complete, in one year (or nine months). Third grade boys and girls also each have a book to complete in one year. The courses of study for fourth, fifth, and sixth grade boys and girls are described in two handbooks, one for boys and one for girls. The older children's study is planned as a three-year program; however, hard-working children may complete the program more quickly.

Each portion of the curricula for younger children is independent of the rest—and the curricula for older children is independent of the younger program. This means that a third grade child may begin and complete the third grade curricula, without having completed the second grade course of study. Also, children may join the Caravan program in the older division without having participated on the younger level. To complete the entire course of study, however, late starters will be required to work on achievements more quickly than those who begin in the fourth grade.

To encourage regular progress in the Caravan program, various stages of advancement are planned for within the two programs. These requirements for advancement include activities and study in five areas for younger children and in four areas for older children. As incentives for learning and participation, awards have been designed.

The program for second grade children includes completion of a number of requirements for becoming a member of the Maiden or Brave wigwams, completion of Deeds of Honor work, completion of eight activities for each of the mental, spiritual, social, physical, and outdoor trophies, and completion of a catechism study for "I Believe" emblems.

The program for sixth graders includes completion of requirements for becoming a member of the Pathfinder or

Trailblazer groups, completion of 11 requirements for attaining the first ranks of Cabin Helper and Sentry; completion of four achievements and four weeks of daily Bible reading for attaining the Camp Keeper and Scout ranks; completion of five achievements and six weeks of daily Bible reading for attaining the Homemaker and Ranger ranks; completion of six achievements for the Fanny Crosby and John Wesley international honor citations; completion of seven achievements for the Helen Keller and David Livingstone honor citations; completion of seven achievements and performance of service to the church for the Florence Nightingale and George Washington Carver honor citations; completion of the Articles of Faith, and completion of seven achievements and performance of service to the church for the Esther Carson Winans and Phineas F. Bresee citations, the highest awards in the Caravan program.

The course of study and activity for primary children is specific, with little opportunity for choice of activity, except for cases where children are instructed to complete 12 of 14 Deeds of Honor and 8 of 10 activities for a trophy achievement. In the junior division, however, children are required to study only 12 specific achievement projects out of a total of 67 which are needed to complete the entire program. The junior handbooks contain 96 choices for achievements and set deadlines by which work is to be completed. Achievement work is completed during regular weekly meetings; at special meetings such as field trips, hikes, and outings; and at home.

Meetings

Regular weekly meetings are scheduled at various times, depending upon the local church program. Most commonly, meetings are scheduled for Wednesday evenings, while adults are involved in the midweek prayer and praise services or other activities. Other options are Saturday mornings or after school on weekdays. Meetings need to be at least 60 minutes long, preferably 90 minutes. They include opening ceremonies, devotions, prayer, achievement work, refreshments, assignments, and an optional closing ceremony.

A year of activities usually involves the nine months of the public school year; however, many programs are operated year round. Since children have more free time during the summer vacation months, Caravan can become a summer ministry; or it can meet at least once a month to keep interest alive.

How to Start a Caravan Ministry

1. Obtain approval from your Children's Council to examine and/or begin the Nazarene Caravan program and to purchase a Caravan Starter Kit or the CST text, *The Caravan Ministry*. These explain in detail the objectives of the program and procedures for operating it.

2. Order from the Nazarene Publishing House the Caravan Starter Kit or the CST text, *The Caravan Ministry*.

3. Appoint a director for the Caravan program, and select a group of persons interested in ministering to children through this program.

4. Complete the CST course, "Developing Caravan Leaders," unit 513b, in class study or in individual study through the Home Study Plan.

5. Register the Caravan program with your district Caravan director and with the general Caravan office at International Headquarters of the Church of the Nazarene, 6401 The Paseo, Kansas City, MO 64131. The Caravan program is organized under the office of Special Ministries in the Department of Children's Ministries, in the Division of Christian Life.

6. Make a one-year schedule of activities. Include registration day, award ceremonies, achievement work, special days, and workers' meetings.

The cost of running a Caravan program is about $5.00 per year per child (this varies some from year to year). This includes the expense of handbooks and uniforms (caps, scarves, and sashes). Expenses can be met in a variety of ways: registration fees, weekly dues and offerings, or special money-raising projects.

The Local Caravan Director

The local Caravan director:

1. Is the Nazarene Caravan program representative on the Children's Council.

2. Arranges with the council a time for the weekly Caravan meeting and other special activities.

3. Presents to the council a budget for operating the Caravan program. This should include handbooks, uniforms, badges, and other supplies.

4. Places an order for Caravan materials to the Nazarene Publishing House.

5. Registers the Caravan group when it is first organized with the general Caravan office in the office of Special Ministries, the Department of Children's Ministries in Kansas City.

6. Makes contact with his district Caravan director for information on special district functions and dates and advises the council.

7. Is the chief promotion person, advertising special functions, an annual registration date, and quarterly award ceremonies.

8. Is the leader and organizer of all activities, including scheduling of weekly meetings and special activities for the entire year.

9. Chooses a staff to carry out the Caravan program and has it approved by the children's council.

10. Leads the various group guides in planning for each weekly meeting and in scheduling of work for the entire year.

11. Acts as the resource person for each group guide and helps schedule specialists for each.

12. Conducts quarterly meetings with the guides and other Caravan helpers.

13. Visits regularly each group and participates in devotions, singing, and games.

14. Leads all award ceremonies.

15. Plans for training of new workers, using the CST course, "The Challenge of Caravan" and its text, *The Caravan Ministry,* or the Home Study Plan.

16. Makes an annual report to the council on Caravan activities, accomplishments, and participation.

Enlisting Help for the Caravan Program

As we indicated earlier, not everyone involved in the Caravan program needs to give full-time service. Because Caravan achievements cover such a wide range of activities in various fields, you can use short-term as well as long-term teachers and helpers.

To acquaint the members of your church with the kinds of help you can use, prepare a form something like the one illus-

---

HELP WANTED

The children of our church are involved in a great number of activities and learning experiences in the Nazarene Caravan Program. If your vocation or hobby appears below, your help can be used for one or two nights during the year. Please check the areas in which you have interests. Our Caravan leaders will be contacting you in regard to scheduling your help.

Games_____	Birds_____	Leathercraft_____
Picnic_____	Fire Prevention_____	Pioneering_____
Wiener Roast_____	Embroidery_____	Rocks_____
Manners_____	Child Care_____	Swimming_____
Cooking_____	First Aid_____	Wood Carving_____
Party_____	Etiquette_____	Agriculture_____
Bible Study_____	Photography_____	Airplanes_____
Crafts_____	Hiking_____	Architecture_____
Animals_____	Fishing_____	Art_____
Health_____	Treasure Hunt_____	Astronomy_____
Campfire_____	Archery_____	Business_____
Collections_____	Athletics_____	Designing_____
Outdoors_____	Automobile_____	Environment_____
Bike Riding_____	Basketry_____	Flowers_____
Horseback Riding_____	Camping_____	Literature_____
Roller-skating_____	Carpentry_____	Music_____
Field Trips_____	Gardening_____	Nature Study_____
Exploring Trip_____	Knots_____	Outdoor Cooking_____
Physical Education_____	Leather Craft_____	Radio_____
Citizenship_____	Missions_____	Space_____
Weather_____	Churchmanship_____	Sewing_____
Coin Collecting_____	Nursing_____	Other_____

NAME_____ Phone_____

ADDRESS_____

trated, listing subject areas in which pupils will be completing achievement badges. Ask members to check areas where they would be willing to share their interests and knowledge. Emphasize the fact that for each area checked, only one, two, or three weeks' involvement would be required.

After you have collected the forms, organize the names and information, then contact your volunteer specialists. Give them

---

CARAVAN ENROLLMENT HAPPENING

For All Second, Third, Fourth, Fifth, and Sixth Graders

September ___, 19__

Dear Parents:

We are organizing the Nazarene Caravan Program for the coming year and will begin with a Caravan Enrollment Happening. The happening will be a week from this coming Friday evening; it will begin at 6:30 and will end at 8:30. Each child should bring wieners and buns.

At this happening we will be demonstrating what happens at Caravan meetings, and we will be enrolling children for the 1980-81 year. When you bring your child, or return for him, there will be forms for you to complete.

The Caravan program is a weekday ministry of the church which seeks to develop children mentally, physically, socially, and spiritually. The program is designed for children in the second, third, fourth, fifth, sixth grades.

Sincerely,

CARAVAN ENROLLMENT FORM

Name_____

Address_____

City_____State_____Zip_____

Age_____

Grade in School_____

Have you been in Caravan before?

_____

If so, what group?_____

If Pathfinder or Trailblazer, what rank?

_____

What parts of the Caravan uniform do you have?_____

_____._____

FOR OFFICE USE

Silver Moon_____

Pocahontas _____

Brave   _____

Chief   _____

Pathfinder _____

Trailblazer_____

Child Needs

Hat   _____

Scarf   _____

Sash   _____

Handbook   _____

copies of the activities they will be teaching; use the exact information given in the Caravan handbooks so that the children will receive the information or complete the projects needed to meet their requirements. Assign each specialist a time when he will be helping in Caravan; then be sure to remind him a week or two in advance of the actual date. Using a wide variety of short-term helpers like this greatly enriches the child's Caravan experiences.

Caravan Specials Plan Sheet

Activity Emphasis_____Date_____

_____

_____

How it will meet requirements for:

Maiden Silver Moon	Maiden Pocahontas	Brave Hunter	Brave Chief	Pathfinder	Trailblazer

Materials and Supplies:

Helpers and Their Responsibilities:

Use Special Events to Spark Your Caravan Ministry

In addition to weekly meetings, there are a variety of special events you can use to enhance your Caravan program. Start off with a bang in the fall with a Caravan Enrollment Event. Announce it with posters and with a letter to parents like the one below. At the event, involve children in one or more activities similar to those that are part of the Caravan program. Later on, sign up the children in the program, using a form similar to the one below. And of course, be sure to serve refreshments!

Once a month or quarter during the coming year, plan additional special events, such as a camp-out, a missions fair, or a craft fair. Design these activities so that as the children are participating in the special, they are also meeting requirements for badges. A form like the Caravan Specials Plan Sheet will help as you prepare for these events.

The possibilities for involving children in exciting learning activities are almost limitless in the Caravan program. For additional helpful information on organization and activities, check the Caravan section of *Kaleidoscope.*

Resources

Teachers' Guidebooks: *The Brave Guide*
The Maiden Guide
The Trailguide
The Pathguide

Pupils' Handbooks: *Hunter*
Chief
Silver Moon
Pocahontas
Trailblazer
Pathfinder

Leaders' Helps: Caravan Starter Kit
The Caravan Ministry,
Bill Young

II. Nazarene Children's Quizzing Program

Children's quizzing provides elementary-age boys and girls with the opportunity for concentrated verse-by-verse study of selected portions of the Bible. There are three goals for children's quizzing. They are to help the child (1) increase his Bible knowledge, (2) want to study the Bible, and (3) learn how to study the Bible. Because the purpose of quizzing is Bible study, as many children as possible should be involved in the program.

At the end of the year's study, the children have the option of beginning preparation for quiz competition. However, it is vitally important to remember that participating in competition is an end-of-the-year extra—not the reason for, nor the ultimate goal of, a children's quiz program. Even if you decide not to compete in zone or district quizzing, you will have already achieved the objective of the program—Bible study. The decision not to compete is not a sign that the leader was a failure, nor a reflection on parents, nor an indication of the smartness or dumbness of the children. Competition is an experience which many children enjoy; but it is not necessary to a successful quiz ministry.

If you decide to compete in zone quizzing—and hopefully qualify for district competition—keep in mind that winning the competition is not a clear-cut sign of how much the children have learned. In many districts a winner is selected on the basis of only three sets of questions. This limited number of questions may not serve as a true indicator of what the children have learned during the past year. Win or lose, children can feel proud of their accomplishments in Bible study. For these reasons, Bible study during the year should never be sacrificed for just rote memorization of the questions and answers in the book. While quiz competition is interesting and exciting, always remember that it is subordinate to Bible study. It is the Bible study which gives the true value to the program.

Organization and Curriculum of the Quiz Program

Children in grades one through six may participate in children's quizzing on two levels.

Boys and girls in grades one and two participate in a pre-quizzing program. This is designed especially to help young children learn about the divisions of the Bible, increase their basic information about the Bible, and develop the Bible skills they will need to participate in regular quizzing later on. First and second graders should not be involved in quiz competition.

Children in grades three through six participate in the regular quiz/Bible study program, which consists of a four-year curriculum cycle. During the four years, quizzers will complete studies in Genesis, Exodus, Matthew, and Acts. While doing concentrated Bible study, they also learn Bible study skills and develop the habit of Bible study. Children in the regular quiz program have the option of taking part in quiz competition.

Why are there two divisions in the quiz program? Because children in grades one and two generally do not have the necessary skills (primarily, advanced reading ability) to participate in verse-by-verse Bible study. For this reason, they should not be involved in the regular quiz program or in competition. This is a significant change from the policy of previous years when first and second graders were allowed though not encouraged to quiz along with older children.

Since young children cannot really take part in the Bible study portion of the program, the only way to involve them is through rote drill and memorization of Bible quiz questions and answers. This puts tremendous pressure on the youngsters —and their parents—and takes the major emphasis away from Bible study and places it on competition. While there may be a few advanced second graders who could enjoy the entire quiz program—Bible study included—this would be an exception. Therefore, it is best to adhere to the policy of allowing only third through sixth graders to be a part of regular quizzing. Making younger children wait will also give stature to the program by making the older participants feel that this is something a little more "grown-up."

How to Begin a Children's Quizzing Program in the Local Church

After the Children's Council has made the decision to begin the quizzing ministry, and has secured the approval of the Board of Christian Life, take these steps to activate your program.

1. Select a local director of children's quizzing. The director will serve on the local Children's Ministries Council.

2. Help the local director become familiar with his job description as given in this chapter. Any points of confusion should be cleared up as soon as possible.

3. Order the materials needed from the Nazarene Publishing House. The quiz director should be involved in this process.

Once these steps have been taken, the quiz director is ready to begin planning and publicizing the program. He should:

1. Work through the entire quiz study, making notes and planning his presentations, following suggestions in the Leader's Guide. Complete guidance for Bible study is given there.

2. Determine the length of time children will spend in study, and set the starting and completion dates for the Bible study. The Leader's Guide gives helpful hints for setting up a study schedule.

3. Publicize the quiz program through posters, announcements, and the weekly church letter. Be sure that everyone knows the time, place, and date you will begin the quiz ministry.

4. Set realistic goals and rewards for accomplishments. Children who participate in quizzing may receive the Bible study achievement in the Caravan program.

What Happens During Quiz Bible Study?

Many different things. Primarily, the children are helped each week to study and review a particular Bible passage or passages. To do this, the Leader's Guide suggests a wide variety of study techniques to help children (1) become acquainted with the Bible material; (2) understand what it means; (3) improve their Bible study skills; and (4) test their recall of what they have studied.

The pupil book is the basic tool for the pupil's study; however, the leader should not rely solely on this. The Leader's Guide suggests extra activities, using other resources. The quiz director should make every effort to enrich the Bible study by using materials such as pictures from Sunday school teaching resource packets, commercial Bible games, Bible word cards, and books about Bible lands and customs.

An important part of quiz Bible study is to help pupils test their recall of what has been learned. This serves two purposes (1) it helps pupils and leaders discover whether the teaching/learning process has been successful; and (2) it helps children become familiar with competition procedures before they actually participate in competition. Brief practice quizzes are provided both in the Leader's Guide and in the pupil books. These should be used regularly, even if your children do not plan to enter zone and district competition.

Rules for Quiz Competition

Complete rules for quizzing are provided in the Leader's Guide, so they are discussed only briefly here. However, the rules given here and in the Leader's Guide are only suggestions. Many of them can be interpreted in two different ways. They have purposely been written that way so districts can tailor the children's quizzing ministry to their specific needs.

The official rules used during your zone and district competition will be those that your District Council of Children's Ministries adopts. Therefore, as you prepare to enter competition, it is important that you contact your district children's quizzing director for the specific rules that will be used on your district.

There may be times when you do not like a particular rule which has been established by your district. If this happens, talk with the district director; he may be able to help you better understand the rule—and he will certainly want to know about your personal feelings. Since the rules are made for one year only, no rule is permanent. There is a chance for change in the next year. In the meantime, be sure to support your district quiz director and Council of Children's Ministries. This is the only way to build a more effective children's quizzing ministry in your district.

Quiz Teams

A quiz team consists of four members and an alternate.

Each district determines the number of teams a church may enter in the zone quiz. Current rules suggest that a church may enter one team for each 75 children in the local congregation, based on the number shown in the most recent district minutes. Winning zone teams go to the district quiz.

Competition Methods

There are two basic methods of competition—the regular method and the alternate method.

Regular Method: The team quizzes as a team. The accumulative team scores determine the winning team. The bonus points can be added to the team score or to the captain's score; the result is the same in either case.

Alternate Method: Each quizzer quizzes on an individual basis. Quizzers still sit together as a team, and the captain still answers bonus questions. However, bonus points are added only to the team score, not to the captain's score. Winners are determined by the highest individual scores.

Some districts use a combination of these two methods. For example, one district selects the top five quizzers from each zone to represent that zone at the district competition. It also awards a special trophy to the church with the top-scoring team. Another district selects the top-scoring team at the zone competition to be the zone entry at the district quiz. The top five quizzers, not on the winning team, may compete on an individual basis at the district for the "Top Quizzer" award.

Regardless of the method or combination of methods used to select a zone and district team, it is suggested that each district use double elimination; that is, each team may lose twice before being eliminated from the competition.

Competition Questions

All questions used in quiz competition have a series of four answers. The Answer Box used by quizzers contains four cards numbered 1, 2, 3, and 4. When the quizmaster calls "Answer," each child pulls up the number he believes is the correct response to that question. Points are awarded for each correct answer.

Official Zone and District Questions are secured from the Children's Quizzing Office in Kansas City. To ensure fairness to all, questions are sent *only* to the district quiz director.

Questions used in a zone or district quiz are drawn from two sources: old questions that pupils have previously encountered in their study books or in a previous zone quiz; and new questions. A new question can be any of the following:

1. A question and set of answers not in the pupil book. Although the pupil has encountered the material in his Bible study, the exact question is not in pupil materials and was not used in zone competition.

2. A question that has been reworded but still has the same answer

3. A question from the pupil's study book which has reworded or renumbered answers

In zone competition, half of the questions used are from the pupil materials and half are new questions. In district competition, some questions come from the study book, some from the sets of zone questions, and some are new questions.

Preparing for Quiz Competition

As stated before, quiz competition is not the focal point of quiz Bible study. However, it can be an interesting and motivating challenge for children if it is approached right. If your church decides to enter competition, follow these steps to prepare your children for it.

1. Secure from the district director the rules that will be used in your district. Become familiar with the rules. Find out from the district director the dates for zone and district competition.

2. Select the best quizzers to represent your church at the zone quiz. If a child who is not ready for competition is allowed to compete, he may come away with feelings of inferiority and frustration because "he lost." He may also lose interest in quizzing—and in Bible study.

You can make team selections in one of these ways: (1) have the local director choose the team; (2) keep scores for the entire year and select the team on the basis of performance and improvement; (3) have a local quiz competition among the children who want to compete for positions on the church team. In this case, the top five scoring quizzers will become the local church team.

Never force an unwilling child to participate in competition. Encourage him if you feel he has the ability, but let the final decision be his. If you have more children who want to compete than the rules allow, you should still involve them in some way. Give them meaningful assignments to help you and the other team members prepare for competition. Depending upon age and abilities, these extras may be used to practice quizzing against the regular team, to keep score, and to help enforce the competition rules.

Be sure also that you recognize every child who has worked hard in the quiz Bible study program. A certificate of completion of the Bible study is included in the pupil books. You might also want to make some other award, such as a Bible study trophy or a gift.

3. Lead the team in concentrated practice, following the quiz regulations. Regular—and correct—practice is important for two reasons. First, children need to realize that just as athletes who are training for competition must sometimes train rather than doing something they would prefer, there will be times when they must sacrifice some activities to study and practice in order to be ready for quizzing competition. Self-discipline is difficult to achieve. But it can make the difference between doing well in competition and doing poorly. If there are areas of study that have been particularly difficult, review this material and answer the children's questions.

Second, practicing by the rules helps the children to be more relaxed during competition. Because they know the rules well, they can concentrate on answering questions.

4. Plan invitational quizzes with other churches, prior to zone competition. These help prepare the children psychologically as well as mentally. With the churches involved, decide on a date, place, and time, and on the amount of material to be covered.

5. At all times, demonstrate and encourage pupils to show a proper attitude toward quizzing competition. This is sometimes difficult to do. We want to encourage children to study

hard and do their best; but at the same time, we must avoid any indication of pressure which says, "You must win at all costs." It is a terrible thing for a team—under pressure—to cheat in order to win a Bible quiz. Parents and leaders in the quiz program must model a proper attitude by remaining relaxed and by emphasizing the fact that winning or losing is not a life-and-death matter. Everyone wants to win; but someone must lose. The important goals of quizzing are good Bible study and an atmosphere of enjoyment in competition.

If the team or selected quizzers make it to district competition, you will be sent a copy of the zone questions. Review these with the quizzers, along with material from the book.

Resources

Quizzing Resources: Pre-Quizzing Program
Children's Quiz Leader's Edition
Children's Quiz Pupil's Book
Answer Box
Score Sheets
Kaleidoscope

III. MISSION EDUCATION FOR CHILDREN

Bernice looked steadily at the dollar bill she held in her hand. She had earned it by being patient, brave, and good during a long and rather painful dental procedure. She was going to use it to buy a jackknife—something she had wanted to own for some time. But now she wondered. As she sat in church, listening to the missionary speaker tell about people in Africa who had never heard of Jesus, she felt within her a growing desire to help. It was a difficult decision, for Bernice seldom received so much money; but when the offering basket was passed, her dollar was among others that had lovingly been given to God for use in missionary work.

Wanda gave one last apprehensive look up the dusty

stairs. Cautiously she began to climb them. How she hated those stairs, leading to the Junior Missionary Society meeting room. They were so dark, and there were spiders in every corner. Wanda was terrified of spiders, but despite her fear she seldom missed junior missionary meeting. Although her teacher had little in the way of curriculum materials, when she told about Africa, Japan, or China, the people and places came alive. When she prayed for the nationals and the missionaries, tears of concern poured down her cheeks.

Do these sound like fiction stories out of a Sunday school paper? Perhaps—but both stories are true. And there is more to them. When Bernice grew up, she became NWMS president in her local church. It wasn't long until her missionary vision began to rub off on others in the society. One day a woman came to Bernice with a sum of money. "Take it," she said. "I was going to buy a new coat this year, but I can wait. Our missionaries need supplies more than I need a coat." It was all Bernice could do to take the money—for her friend truly did need a new coat. But she knew, from personal experience, the motive that had prompted the action.

And Wanda? She, too, retained the burden for missions which she had absorbed as a child. When she was grown, she and her husband, Sidney Knox, went to New Guinea to pioneer Nazarene missions in that country. Today, Wanda is the head of Nazarene World Missionary Society, an organization which—in partnership with the Department of Children's Ministries—is vitally concerned about the missionary education of today's children.

Christ made it very plain in the New Testament that missions is not an option for the Church. Every Christian is included in the commission, "Go ye" (Matt. 28:19, KJV). Some may not go far—geographically. Their outreach to non-Christians may be confined to "Jerusalem"—their hometown. Others may have opportunities to witness further—"in all Judaea, and in Samaria, and unto the uttermost part of the earth" (Acts 1:8, KJV). But all who share Christ with others are doing missionary work. Furthermore, those who cannot go to other places to minister can be involved actively in supportive missionary work—praying for and giving to those who do go. And missionary involvement is not limited to adults only; children can also be actively involved in missions.

Nazarene missionary education for children has three major goals: (1) to inform children about our Nazarene missionary work around the world; (2) to inspire children to want to participate in missionary work by modeling for them both concern for and sacrificial effort in behalf of missions; and (3) to involve children in missionary work. Let's look more closely at how these goals may be accomplished.

Informing Children About Missions

The Church of the Nazarene provides a variety of materials designed to help inform children about missionary work. These include (1) Sunday school lessons about missions; (2) an annual VBS missionary emphasis; (3) the annual Children's Missionary Packet; and (4) six annual missionary reading books—three for younger children and three for older children.

Kindergarten, primary, middler, and junior Sunday school curriculum cycles each contain at least one—sometimes more— missionary units. In these, the children study the biblical basis for missions and learn some specific facts about Nazarene missions in various countries.

Each year in VBS, a special missionary project is emphasized. VBS materials contain a set of colorful posters, plus a leader's guide of instructions, telling about a particular phase of both home missions and world missions.

The annual Children's Missionary Packet is a complete curriculum based on the outline of study prescribed by the Department of World Mission and the NWMS. The packet contains a leader's guide of 12 lessons, Ditto masters for individual handwork, a map, posters, and other helpful materials which vary from year to year. The packet can be used in a variety of settings, which will be discussed later.

Six missionary books, designed to be read by or to children, are produced each year to correlate with the church missionary emphasis. These books present both historical information about missions and facts about missionary work today in home and world areas. Children who read the books are counted as "missionary readers," just as are the adults who read the adult missionary books.

Each of the above sources provides children with a wealth of information about Nazarene missions. They learn about the customs of various countries, the missionaries who work there, and the needs of both the missionaries and the nationals. Through these materials we seek also to inspire children to become actively involved in missions.

Inspiring Children

As we saw from the stories of Bernice and Wanda, hearing about the needs of missions is one way of inspiring children to want to be a part of missionary work. But this is not enough. Although some have said, "When we know, we care,"[1] inspiration comes from other sources, too. One of the most valuable of these is the example of the adults with whom the child associates.

Children in the church need to see adults actively caring for others and doing their part in missionary work. What will they notice about the response of adults in your church to such things as (1) visitation and calling? (2) missionary conventions? (3) special missionary offerings? (4) urgent prayer needs from the mission field? If the prevailing attitude is one of indifference, it will be difficult to inspire children to care much about missions. But if it is one of concern and enthusiastic effort, children will "catch" and reproduce this attitude. And once children are inspired to help, it is usually not difficult to involve them willingly in missionary work.

Involving Children

The materials provided for mission education of children give you the resources to involve children in missionary effort of various kinds.

Sunday school materials encourage children to pray for missionaries by name, and to give an offering for an approved special. The amounts raised by the children are gratifying— sometimes up into thousands of dollars. The curriculum materials give suggestions for helping children earn and raise money for missions. In addition, projects are often suggested to encourage children to become directly involved in reaching out to those close to them.

The annual VBS offering is another opportunity for children to raise money for missions. Colorful posters help them become aware of a specific need, both in world and in home missions. The offering they bring is equally divided between the World and Home Missions departments. VBS directors are encouraged to report to the children each year how much was raised the previous year, and how the money was used to help others.

During the year's study using the Children's Missionary Packet, children are given frequent opportunities to participate in missionary work—through prayer, giving, and special projects.

Where and When to Teach Missions

In addition to Sunday school and VBS, missionary education can occur in these settings, using the Children's Missionary Packet.

Children's Church. Many churches present missionary lessons either once a month or as short units of study during children's church. This second option is probably better for several reasons, of which the two major ones are given here. First, when missionary lessons are presented in units, pupils receive a greater continuity in their study. This method also prevents regular children's church units from being interrupted every four weeks for the missionary lesson.

Sunday Evenings. This allows for more informal programming, which is ideal for in-depth studies of missions. With more time and in an informal setting, you can be more creative in the use of learning centers and special activities (such as cooking a food from a particular country).

Caravan. Since some of the achievement badges in Caravan are related to missions, this makes a good time to present mission study. Also, this is often the time that the adults are having their study.

Special Missionary Emphases

Children should be given regular instruction in missions, but they should be involved also in the special missions events of the church, such as missionary conventions, mission jamborees, and even church missionary projects.

Resources

Children's Missionary Packet
Primary reading books
Junior reading books
Kaleidoscope

Reference Note

1. John T. Sizemore, *The Ministry of Religious Education* (Nashville: Broadman Press, 1978), p. 99.

A child needs meadows to explore
Where daisy faces nod,
And quiet times of wonderment
To think his thoughts of God.
                    —KATHRYN B. PECK

9

Annual and Special Ministries

Turn Back the Time Machine

If we could look into the past and view even a few historic moments in the Christian education of children, what would we discover? Let's take a look and see.

1866—First Church of Boston feels the need to provide religious instruction for children in the summertime. They organize the first known Bible school for that purpose.

1877—Christians in Montreal, Quebec, launch a full summer program for children consisting of hymns, songs, Bible reading, memory work, military drills, calisthenics, manual work, and patriotic exercises.

1894—A Methodist pastor's wife in Hopedale, Ill., establishes a Bible school for children of her town. Forty children, graded in four departments, attend.

1898—Mrs. Eliza Hawes, a Baptist Sunday school teacher, becomes worried about the scores of children who roam the streets of New York City with nothing to do. She asks her pastor's permission to bring the children to the church for instruction. The church catches the vision of the project and works with her to establish an "Everyday Bible School." Two hours each day, for six weeks, the children meet for flag salutes, worship, Bible stories, drawing and games, memorization, nature study, and, for the girls, cooking and sewing.

1901—Robert G. Boville, administrator of a Baptist mission, wonders, "Why can't idle children, idle churches, and idle teachers be brought together in a number of Bible schools?" The result? The organization of several such schools and the beginning of the modern Bible school movement.[1]

These and other such incidents illustrate the fact that for many years concerned Christians have seen the need to expand their Bible teaching opportunities with children. The results? Today, almost every church provides—or supports—Christian education experiences such as vacation Bible school and camping. In the Church of the Nazarene, these are known as *annual ministries*. In addition to these, there are a number of additional means of reaching and teaching children known in our church as *special ministries*. In this chapter, we will consider the unique contributions of each of these two groups of ministries.

I. ANNUAL MINISTRIES

What Are Annual Ministries?

Annual ministries are those ministries provided by the Department of Children's Ministries which occur once a year, usually in the summer. This choice of time for the scheduling of annual ministries is not because "there's no other time left," but because the summer offers some unique potential for ministry not found at other times of the year. In the summer, boys and girls are out of school. They generally have much more free time—large chunks of time—available to them than they do during the remainder of the year. The opportunity to minister to children in these longer, undivided portions of time is one of the key factors in the popularity and success of annual ministries—VBS and camping. Rather than meeting with children in short half-hour to hour-and-a-half sessions once a week, either on Sunday or a weekday, annual ministries provide children with intensive, concentrated times of Bible study, worship, fellowship, and service opportunities.

A. Vacation Bible Schools

Vacation Bible school is a church-sponsored school providing Christian instruction for children (and often teens and adults) during a part of the summer vacation. The strengths of the VBS and the unique possibilities for ministry are many.

1. VBS provides a time of concentrated study. Although today's schools have become considerably shorter than the early ones cited at the beginning of this chapter, most offer a minimum of 12½ to 15 hours of instruction (2½ to 3 hours a day for a week) and sometimes up to 25 or 30 hours. This concentration of study involves more than just the accumulative number of hours. It also means that it is much easier to build one concept upon another, because the children do not have an entire week between sessions to forget what they learned before. This concentration also affects evangelistic opportunities in a similar way. The instructional and emotional buildup leading to a decision is not dissipated by long time periods between invitations.

2. VBS gives children a well-balanced diet of instruction, worship, fellowship, and service opportunities. Although all of these elements are available in varying amounts in other ministries, VBS combines all four in the week or two-week program.

3. Evangelism is an important feature of the VBS—and, as we mentioned before, it is often more effective because of the concentrated time together.

4. VBS gives a church a wonderful opportunity for outreach into the community. Although there are still hundreds of VBSs being held in churches, a growing number have moved out of the four walls into the backyards. When the VBS is succeeded by careful and intensive follow-up, new inroads into unchurched families are often the result.

Financing and Planning for VBS

Although it is a once-a-year experience, and is generally held in the summer, VBS needs to be a vital part of the total church plans and financing. The cost of the VBS should be written into the annual church budget, not left to be paid for by offerings which the children bring. The children will bring money; but this should be used for the VBS missionary offering, rather than to defray the cost of the school. If careful records are kept from year to year, the church will know about how much to set aside for the work of VBS.

At least six months before the summer, the VBS director should be selected and the VBS dates established. It takes four to six months to plan a good VBS. Nazarene VBS materials are available by January 1, so this makes a good time to begin planning, organizing, and ordering curriculum materials.

The Work of the Local VBS Director

The individual who is the key to the success of the VBS is the local VBS director. Although this person must be fully supported by the pastor, and by a complete staff of age-level teachers, helpers, and activity specialists, he or she is the one who plans and administers all of the work that is done. The tasks of the VBS director are as follows.

The VBS director:

1. Is the VBS representative on the Children's Council.
2. Conducts planning sessions with the pastor, chairman of the Board of Christian Life, director of children's ministries, and the Children's Council to enlist and place all VBS workers.
3. Conducts a training program for workers. Studies church facilities and assigns space. Encourages all workers to attend district and/or zone VBS workshops.
4. Submits a budget plan to the Children's Council.
5. Orders all supplies and curriculum.
6. Holds planning sessions with the pastor, chairman of the Board of Christian Life, and director of children's ministries to promote VBS in the church and advertise it in the community.
7. Conducts supervisors' planning sessions and workshop preparation meetings.
8. Makes personal contacts with Sunday school classes or departments to help stimulate interest in VBS.
9. Conducts promotion and visitation campaigns.
10. Arranges for pupil enrollment, in advance if possible.
11. Holds planning conferences with student helpers, safety patrol, sports captains, ushers, hostesses, and/or others.
12. Plans with the pastor for a public service of dedication.
13. Directs the vacation Bible school.
14. Conducts the follow-up program to conserve results.

a. Gives all names of unchurched pupils to the pastor, Sunday school teachers, chairman of the Board of Christian Life, director of children's ministries, and visitation groups.

b. Visits all new prospects.

15. Looks ahead to the next year by packing away all usable materials.

16. Expresses by word or letter appreciation for all the workers.

17. Completes permanent records and submits reports.

What Kind of VBS Shall We Have?

An important first step in planning a VBS is to determine the general format of the school. In the past, most vacation Bible schools were held at the church which sponsored it. Outreach into the community was made (1) by word of mouth of the church children or parents; (2) through door-to-door canvassing of communities near the church; and (3) occasionally by bussing in children from other communities. The school of this type met in the morning for about 2½ hours a day for 10 days and was known as the "standard school."

In recent years, the traditional two-week, at-the-church, daytime VBS has declined in popularity. There are several reasons for this. First, many mothers work and can no longer help out in a daytime VBS. Second, churches have wondered how effective an at-the-church VBS was in reaching out to unchurched homes. Third, more and more people find it difficult to devote two full weeks to VBS because of the pressures of work schedules, public school summer sessions, longer vacations, and the like. For these reasons, many churches are now taking an optional approach to scheduling and holding VBS.

A complete description of all VBS options is provided for you in the book *VBS: A Creative Summer Ministry*, by Jeannette Wienecke. Here is a brief summary of some of them.

Evening VBS. In some cases, the evening school can solve the problem of obtaining staff; those who work and cannot teach in a day school are able to help out in the evening school. The major drawback of the evening school is that this is a less suitable time of day for preschoolers, who tire easily. However, if plenty of rest time is provided, this option usually works well.

Day Camp VBS. A day camp is a week of all-day activity in an outdoor setting, such as a Girl or Boy Scout camp, public park, state park, outlying farm, or nature refuge. In most cases, the children come to the church and are bussed to and from the day camp site. The children bring a sack lunch, or a lunch is provided by the church.

In a day camp VBS, the vacation Bible school curriculum is used, but the entire VBS program can be greatly expanded. For example:

- The sports program may include such things as archery, riding, swimming, or fishing.
- The craft program can be enriched to include more complicated crafts or several nature crafts.
- A strong emphasis on nature activities is possible.
- Since the program goes all day, there is more time for Bible study, memorization, and worship activities.

The day camp VBS is an appealing option because it provides a way to minister to children in an outdoor setting away from the church.

The 5- or 10-Week VBS. This kind of school is usually run on the church premises, but on any particular day only one age-group is present. For example, preschoolers come on Monday, primaries on Tuesday, middlers on Wednesday, and so on. This option means that workers are involved only 1 day a week, rather than 5 or 10 days in a row. However, the important VBS value of concentrated study is lost.

Another approach to the 5- or 10-session VBS is to have the whole school meet once a week—on Wednesday evening or Saturday. This option has the same values and drawbacks as the other plan.

Satellite VBS. Satellite schools are held by a smaller staff in an outreach location. This may be an inner-city area, or a residential area which the church wishes to "break into." The satellite school acquaints the neighborhood with the school and also gains new prospects which can be brought into the church's ministry. In some instances, the satellite school can be the beginning of a branch Sunday school—but the VBS is held for its own value in ministering to community children.

The Neighborhood Backyard (Garage or Patio) VBS. This type of school is similar to the satellite school but is held at the home of a church member. The sponsoring church generally conducts several backyard schools simultaneously in several different neighborhoods. In some situations, each school serves only one or two age levels; in others, children of all ages are welcome. The backyard school is a particularly effective way of reaching out to unchurched families. The person in whose home the school is held is generally known in the neighborhood and generally helps with visitation and follow-up. After a backyard VBS it is often easier to interest unchurched families in the church.

The Monday Night Family VBS. This option allows families to use VBS materials as part of the "Monday Night Is Family Night" denominational emphasis. Parents receive from the church the age-level materials they need to teach the children in their home. These materials are then used each Monday night throughout the summer. Parents may use the materials as they fit best in their family interests and schedule. This VBS option reduces the need for staff and gives families opportunity to be together. It does limit the possibility of concentrated Bible study because the sessions are a week apart.

Split-Shift VBS. This kind of VBS is helpful in a church where rooms and facilities are limited, because each room can be used up to three times if necessary. The children all attend VBS the same week but at different times. For example, preschoolers attend in the morning; primaries, middlers, and juniors in the afternoon; and teens at night. If staff is limited, some may do double duty, working in two of the three sessions. The major drawback to this plan is the problem of transportation for families in which there are several different ages of children, especially if the family lives some distance from the church.

Mobile VBS. Some churches who want to reach out to the unchurched use a VBS on wheels. They equip a bus, van, or camper with the necessary materials and supplies for Bible school. The mobile unit goes into a new area, using signs and loudspeakers to advertise the school. Workers do such things as give a puppet show and hand out balloons, treats, and invitations to the VBS. Since the invitations must be signed by parents for the child to receive a gift, this gives the school a casual registration and some knowledge of the age-groups they will be serving. However, the school must be flexible and be prepared for variation.

One church has a large bus which holds up to 10 different schools a day, five days a week. The unit has a scheduled day and time, morning or afternoon, at each location. The workers and teachers, as well as all equipment, supplies, visuals, crafts, and refreshments, are transported to each location daily.

At the end of such a VBS it is wise to hold a closing program for parents. This, along with careful records, will provide new prospects for the Sunday school. The mobile unit may also prepare the way for new bus routes.

Monthly VBS. For the church that is short of space and staff, the monthly VBS may be the answer. In June, schedule VBS for primaries and middlers only. Conduct the same type of school for juniors and teens in July. In late August announce "Preschool VBS" to coincide with the "back-to-school" dates for older children. Preschoolers will love "going to school" just like their big brothers and sisters. After the preschool VBS, plan a children's Open House Rally to bring all groups together to share with parents and friends.

A Look at VBS Curriculum

A common question faced by churches as they plan VBS is "Shall we have a 5- or 10-session school?" Opinions vary. Some feel 10 sessions are best and don't even consider fewer. Others, equally concerned, cry, "But we don't have time, staff, or finances for more than 5 sessions."

Adding to the problem was the fact that most VBS materials were written for 10 sessions. Stewardship-conscious church leaders hated to pay for 10 sessions of material and then use only 5. Some attempted to solve this dilemma by using all the material in a one-week school—teaching two sessions each day. This plan did not work well in most cases, especially for preschool children. Children learn best when there is time for repetition of ideas—not an increased number of concepts to learn.

Recognizing that many churches need materials for only 5 sessions, while others still want 10, Nazarene VBS curriculum has been planned to allow for both options. Ten session guides are provided in each of the age-group manuals—but they are based upon only 5 different lesson themes. For each theme, there is a basic, or *core* session, followed by an *expanded* session. Thus, instead of 10 different sessions numbered 1, 2, 3,

. . . 10, the 5 *core* and 5 *expanded* sessions are numbered 1, 1X, 2, 2X, and so forth. Here is how the system works.

In each *core* session, the children are introduced to a new Bible story, Bible verses, and songs, based on a new lesson theme. Detailed procedures for teaching are given, along with complete listings of all materials and supplies needed for that session. There are new materials in the resource packet and pupil book to support each of the *core* sessions.

The *expanded* session which immediately follows each *core* session does exactly what the term suggests. Using the same story, verses, and songs introduced earlier, it continues to develop the theme of the *core* session through a variety of enriching and exciting Bible learning activities. A complete teaching plan for the day is described. However, for teachers who really wish adventure, ideas for even greater creativity and flexibility are given.

A five-session school should use only five session guides— probably the core sessions numbered 1-5. Ten-session schools, on the other hand, will use all *core* and *expanded* sessions.

What are the benefits of this kind of plan? For either the 5- or 10-session school they are many. Consider these.

For the 5-Session School

1. No longer do teachers use only half of the biblical material provided in their manual. A 5-session school teaches the same number of Bible stories, verses, and concepts as the 10-session school. It uses all of the teaching resources and pupil book materials, but without the strain of having to teach two entirely different lessons each day. A 5-session school is limited only in the number of learning activities it can offer to its students and the amount of reinforcement feedback it can incorporate.

2. A five-session school has the added bonus of five resource sections from which to draw in teaching the core sessions in much greater depth. Remember—the *expanded* sessions do not treat five different topics. They describe additional ways to treat the biblical material and concepts introduced in *core* sessions.

Suppose, then, that a teacher would like to substitute an activity from Session 1X for an activity described in Session 1. By all means he should. Teachers should feel free to use any ideas from expanded sessions if they prefer them and feel they would benefit the class.

3. Some teachers might prefer to teach the five expanded sessions by simply adding the Bible story narrative and pupil book activities from corresponding *core* sessions. Expanded sessions are complete enough to do this easily.

4. If you prefer, you may save the expanded sessions for future use. This was not a factor in developing these really new VBS materials, but it is an occasional bonus. By adding Bible stories, verses, and pupil book materials from *core* sessions, you have complete session guides. Use them for children's church, special children's meetings, or for times when child care is provided during adult meetings.

For the 10-Session School

The 10-session school is blessed with a most important commodity in Christian education—time. VBS teachers can reap full benefits from this additional time, using both *core* and *expanded* sessions.

1. You will have time for development, feedback, and reinforcement. This is not repetition of the same idea in the same way. It is repetition of the same basic content in many different and creative ways—through art, field trips, dramatics, games, and crafts. The result is better learning.

2. Teachers will have time in class to explore each concept more deeply. Pupils will have two sessions to live with an idea, look at it from several different angles, experiment, and enjoy learning.

3. Teachers and pupils will have time for all the exciting things they have always wanted to try in VBS but could never fit into the crowded daily schedule. The expanded sessions may be likened to a piece of elastic in a tight belt. They allow both teachers and pupils to breathe and enjoy learning at a viable pace, with more opportunity for creative learning experiences.

4. Teachers can invest their time preparing each idea and resource thoroughly. Because there are only five stories to tell, five verses to learn, and five major concepts to develop, there is time to prepare these in greater depth.

Five sessions or 10? The choice is yours. We hope you can plan for 10 sessions because the opportunities for richer teaching and evangelism are so tremendous. But either way, Nazarene

VBS materials are designed for flexibility to meet your needs and the needs of the children you teach.

Resources

A complete line of graded curriculum for nursery, kindergarten, primary, middler, and junior, including teacher's guides, pupil books, and resource packets, is published annually.

Introductory Packet
Director's Packet
VBS Notebook

B. Let's Go Camping

People today are seeking a dynamic purpose for their lives. They want a faith by which they can live. Church camping can help children find the Christian conviction parents are seeking for themselves. If a boy or girl works, plays, lives, and learns with Christian camp leaders, he can catch from them the joy of their spiritual experiences and their faith. Through these adults he may be led to a deeper appreciation of Jesus, who reveals God and who makes it possible for us to live at our best; to a sense of companionship with Him; and to a feeling that they have a share in the responsibility for helping others to know and love Jesus.

As this statement so beautifully says, the benefits to the child of an experience at a Christian camp are many. Take a closer look at these. The Christian camp:

1. Provides the child with an opportunity to live in God's out-of-doors. Children are growing up in a mechanized and materialistic world. Congested urban metropolitan areas are not conducive to a consciousness of the Creator's presence and to an awareness of His handiworks. A week at camp gives the child an awareness of God's creative power as revealed in the out-of-doors.

2. Offers valuable fellowship with other Christians. Camping is an experience of group living. The impact of life upon life has a more vital and lasting effect than sermons or les-

sons. Learning to give and take, and to demonstrate a concern for the good of others, is built in.

3. Offers a vital Christian atmosphere and program. Everything during the day, whether in chapel or on the trail, has a bearing upon the Christian influence of the camp.

4. Utilizes dedicated Christian leadership. Pastors, youth and children's workers, and Christian lay men and women provide exceptional opportunities for guidance and counsel. The camper can see Christianity as a part of all life through the fellowship with Christian adults.

5. It provides for decisions. Individuals who live in such surroundings frequently make decisions of lasting importance. Conversions, rededications, and surrender for full-time Christian service are among the basic commitments made at camp.

Kinds of Camps

Richard Troup, in the chapter on "Recreation and Camps" from *Childhood Education in the Church,* describes six kinds of camping experiences for children.

Trip Camping. Campers travel by bus or van from site to site. Because of the tedium of travel for children, this type of camp is normally not used extensively with boys and girls.

Trail Camping. On foot, bike, minibike, horse, or canoe, the trail camp moves as a trip camp does, except that it goes by power from the campers. An advantage of both trail and trip camping is that expensive facilities are not needed. Public lands, national seashores, national parks, forests, and other lands contain thousands of miles of developed trails. Maps available from the U.S. Geological Survey and the U.S. Forest Service indicate trails for hikers, bikers, and jeepers. Children enjoy backpack camping with parents and with especially trained leaders doing most of the planning, carrying, cooking, and shelter construction.

Weekend Camping. Some districts have facilities for year-round camping. By including winter and spring school vacations and long weekends, they can add up to 100 days to the usual 90-day summer session. Retreats for families and workshops for church workers are natural events for this kind of camping. If children are present, special activities and programs should be planned for them. Also, older children may participate in these kinds of camps planned especially for them.

Family Camping. In this kind of camping situation, children attend with their parents and participate in activities as a family. Churches can rent facilities and operate their own programs for this kind of camping.

Day Camping. Day camping is ideal for primaries and juniors and can occasionally be adapted to fit the needs of four- and five-year-olds. A day camp operates only during daylight hours. It may operate for a single day, such as a Saturday or any weekday; or it may operate for several days in succession. Children usually bring their own lunch sacks, and the camp provides the drink for lunch; morning and afternoon snacks can be provided by either the camper or the camp. A day camp may be held on the church site, in a city park, on the lawns of large residences, or in county, state, and national parks and forests. With planning, a great number of other sites in and around towns and cities can be developed or used for day camping. With little or no sleeping or eating facilities needed, camping costs are kept at a minimum. With adequate planning, day camping can be self-supporting financially.

Resident Camping. Overnight camps, lasting from five full 24-hour periods to as long as full summer sessions of 10 weeks, have been part of the church's ministry for a century. Usually age-graded, separate sessions are held for middler and junior children. Fees are collected in advance to cover meals, lodging, and materials that are used during the camp. This kind of camp, planned by the district and lasting for five days during the summer, annually involves thousands of children in the Church of the Nazarene. The role of the local church in this type of camp is to (1) promote it by encouraging children to attend, and (2) support the camp by sending volunteer adults to help as counsellors, cooks, or in other camp leadership areas, as requested by the district camp director.

Promoting the Camp Through Summer Camp Savings Plan

In addition to promoting the district children's camps and encouraging children to attend them, local churches can participate in this ministry to their children even more by helping them save money to pay the camp fees. Through a local camp activities director and the Church of the Nazarene summer camp stamp book program, children can save 25 cents at a time until enough money is saved.

Summer Camp Stamp Book. Available from the Nazarene Publishing House is the official Summer Camp Stamp Book. These come in packages of 12, complete with enough camp stamps to fill all 12 books.

The book contains spaces for 200 stamps, an envelope pocket inside the front cover to keep money until the stamps are purchased and attached to the page, and directions to the camper for using the stamp book plan of financing camp fees. When filled, the book is worth $50.00. If cost of the district camp is greater than $50.00, campers will need to begin filling another book. Once the camp fee is reached, they may wish to continue saving for extra spending money at camp.

The cost of the book and the stamps is not recovered when the children purchase the stamps for camp. The cost for each book is assumed by the church as a service to the camper.

Administering the Plan. When the Children's Council chooses to use the stamp book savings plan, a camp activities director should be appointed to administer it. This probably will be the person who is in charge of district camp promotion, pre-registration, and transportation, and who is in charge of any local church camping activities.

In early fall, the camp activities director should determine how many children will be participating in the savings plan. To determine this, he may inform parents of all camp-age children that this savings service is available, and he may request that they indicate to him if their children wish to participate. The information piece may be a flyer that is distributed during Sunday school or children's church, or mailed with the weekly church newsletter. When he knows the correct number, he orders the stamp saving books.

Once the books have been delivered, the director should devise a method of distributing the books and the stamps. He may wish to organize a campaign around the theme: The Camp Stamp Man. Announcements, reminders, a sales booth in the children's department, and even a costume, may be designed with this theme in mind. He will probably want to present a savings plan that encourages a specific amount to be saved each week or month, so the children will not fall short of their goals. So that children put the stamps in the books as quickly as possible after the purchase, the director may require that stamps be sold only if the camper has his book with him. The director should keep a tally on the number of stamps he has sold each child; however, the prime responsibility of pasting the stamps in the books belongs to the camper.

The money which has been collected from the children should be given to the church treasurer. Since many churches use the unified bookkeeping system, the treasurer will put these savings on the church books; however, these funds will be reserved in a special account so that campers can cash in their books at the time of camp registration.

Income to Buy Stamps. Helping children acquire the funds to purchase camp stamps is another service the camping activities director can render. He may suggest to children that they use their allowances to purchase the stamps or with money earned from performing small jobs and tasks for persons in their neighborhoods and in the church body.

Supporting the District Camp

It is the task of the district camp director to recruit counsellors and other camp staff. However, a local camp activities director can be of great help in assisting the district director by suggesting names of those who are qualified and/or interested in helping at camp. Because he generally knows the people of the local church better than does the district director, he is in a better position to name those who: (1) love children and enjoy working with them; (2) have the spiritual qualities needed for effective camp leadership; (3) enjoy life out-of-doors; and (4) have a particular skill which could be shared—even on a short-term basis—with the camp.

The importance of a camp experience for children is great.

Not only do children generally enjoy camping, but many have been led—at camp—to give their lives completely to God.

The general camping office in the Department of Children's Ministries at the Church of the Nazarene headquarters prepares annually a camping packet which is distributed to district camping directors. This packet contains a suggestion for the camp theme and various ways to carry out the theme. These include a curriculum piece and numerous ideas for crafts, and other activities that correlate with the theme.

II. SPECIAL MINISTRIES

What Are Special Ministries?

Special ministries are those ministries of the church which do not fit into Sunday, weekday, or annual time slots. Some, like Cradle Roll or Bible memory, are carried on at many different times during the week and throughout the year. Others, like children's music or reading programs, are not so much separate ministries as they are complements to other programs, such as Sunday school, mission education, or Caravan.

The Church of the Nazarene provides several special ministries to children. These are: Cradle Roll, music and drama, reading, and Bible memorization.

A. Cradle Roll—Ministry to Young Families

Candy Jenkins stared around her trailer home in dismay. In the kitchen were dishes—including lots of baby bottles—to wash. The living room contained scattered piles of clean diapers to fold; and in the laundry room more baby clothes to wash were stacking up. Candy had formula to mix, a bed to make, and supper to fix. But two-week-old Sondra was fussing again—threatening to launch into a full-fledged wail in a few minutes. As Candy went to pick her up, she wondered for the 10th time that day how one sweet, precious baby girl could so totally disrupt a smooth-running household. Did other new mothers have the same problems?

Just then the doorbell rang. When Candy opened the door, she was greeted by a smiling young woman just a few years older than herself. "Mrs. Jenkins," the woman began, "I'm Laura Evans from the Church of the Nazarene, just down the street. My pastor told me that you've just had a new baby, and we'd like to give you a small gift for her. May I come in?"

"I—well, the house—I mean, things are a bit of a mess," stammered Candy. "I just can't seem to get much done these days."

"Don't worry about that," replied Laura with a reassuring smile as she entered the living room. "I know just what you're going through. Why, just a few years ago when my first baby was born, I thought I would come apart at the seams. Here, let me help you fold diapers while we talk."

Forty-five minutes later, Laura patted Candy's hand and Sondra's bottom one more time before she left. Candy was all smiles. "I can't wait to show the bib and these leaflets to my husband Jeff," she said. "And we will try to come to church on Sunday. Thanks so much for all your help!"

Candy, Jeff, and Sondra Jenkins represent thousands of young families who need the ministry of the Cradle Roll. The birth of a new baby—especially the first—adds many pressures to a family. At the same time, young couples are greatly aware of the tremendous responsibilities they face as they guide a young life to maturity. They want to do their best—but many don't know how. At this critical time the Cradle Roll can minister to unchurched families through a program of loving concern and perhaps win both parents and their baby to the church and to the Lord.

Questions and Answers About Cradle Roll

Here are some commonly asked questions about the Cradle Roll and its ministry.

1. What is the Cradle Roll? The Cradle Roll is the program of the church which is concerned with ministry to unchurched parents and their babies (birth through age four). The purpose of the Cradle Roll is outreach—to locate and visit babies and young parents until they are enrolled in the Sunday school, become regular in attendance, and ultimately become responsible born-again Christians. Thus, the Cradle Roll is an effective arm of evangelism; every name on the Cradle Roll list represents parents who may be won to Christ and the church.

2. Who are Cradle Roll members? They are children under

four who do not attend Sunday school and who have been enrolled by a Cradle Roll supervisor or worker. Children remain on the Cradle Roll until they begin to attend Sunday school with some degree of regularity. When this happens, they are taken off the Cradle Roll and are enrolled in the suitable nursery class—crib, toddlers, twos, or threes. From then on they are counted in the Sunday school attendance when present, and the nursery supervisor assumes responsibility for distributing Cradle Roll packet leaflets.

Cradle Roll members are part of the total Sunday school enrollment, just as are Home Department members. However, they should be considered prospects for the Nursery Department. The parents of the children are prospects for the Young Adult Department, or an adult class. Any children on the Cradle Roll who have not started attending Sunday school regularly by their fourth birthday should be transferred to the prospect list of the Kindergarten Department.

3. Why have a Cradle Roll? There are at least three good reasons why an active Cradle Roll is vital—both to parents and children, and to the church.

First, a Cradle Roll program provides excellent prospects for the church visitation program. This gives the church the potential for people in Sunday school and worship.

Second, the Cradle Roll provides a needed ministry to people at a very critical stage of life, and at a time when they are more receptive to spiritual matters. Dan and Cynthia were one such couple. They had married young and had only a nominal church background. Having a good time—no matter in what way—was the major goal of their lives. Then came little Trishia and suddenly life took on a new dimension. Through the Cradle Roll, Dan and Cynthia became interested in the church and occasionally came to the services. One morning, after the preaching service, they made their way to the altar, baby in arms, to give their lives to God. Their concern for their child had opened their hearts to the Lord.

Third, because Cradle Roll means more persons won for Christ it also means more Christian homes for little children. This has far-reaching implications. The possibility of a child's becoming a Christian when he is old enough to do so is greater if the child is raised in a Christian home.

4. What materials are available to use in the Cradle Roll

ministry? The Nazarene Publishing House provides a variety of colorful and informative materials to use with Cradle Roll parents. Three items are particularly important. One is the packet, *First Steps Toward God.* This contains nine leaflets to parents with helpful parenting information, a Cradle Roll certificate, two birthday cards, and a variety of other items.

A second item available is the "Train Up a Child" Calendar. This is especially good to use in families where there are two children in the Cradle Roll. The calendar contains beautiful pictures, helpful information to parents, and scripture verses.

The third major item is the Our Babies chart. Use this at the church to picture and name the children on your Cradle Roll.

5. Who can have a Cradle Roll? Any church, large or small. It takes only one unchurched baby to start a Cradle Roll. Only one worker is needed to begin this ministry. Later, as the program grows, more workers can be added. There are unchurched babies and parents everywhere. It is the challenge of the Cradle Roll to reach these people for the Lord.

The Cradle Roll Supervisor

The first step in beginning a Cradle Roll ministry is to elect a Cradle Roll supervisor. This person is nominated by the pastor and director of children's ministries, and elected by the Board of Christian Life.

It is important to elect the right person to this important task. The Cradle Roll supervisor (as well as all other workers) should be a person who loves and understands babies and small children. Choose a person who has an interest in parents' problems. She must realize the importance of the role of parents and the home during these early crucial years:

—in forming attitudes and behavior which will be patterns continuing into the adult life of the child
—in forming spiritual foundations
—in the unconscious teaching of values
—in giving the child a "sense of worth," the cornerstone of a healthy personality

She must love the Lord with deep devotion and be enthusiastic about the ministry of the Cradle Roll. She should also have tact, patience, and perseverance. She must evidence a willingness to serve God and a desire to see the church grow.

The duties of the Cradle Roll director are as follows.

The local director of Cradle Roll:

1. Is the Cradle Roll representative on the Children's Council.
2. Becomes thoroughly acquainted with the Cradle Roll program of ministry and outreach evangelism.
3. Is always mindful of the total purpose of the Cradle Roll ministry—outreach and evangelism.
4. Assumes responsibility through the Children's Council for complete organization and advancement of the work of the Cradle Roll Department.
5. Cooperates with the pastor and director of children's ministries to recommend assistants.
6. Surveys the field, enrolling babies and presenting enrollment certificates.
7. Works out a visitation program with workers.
8. Keeps records, making sure that nursery and young adult teachers and the pastor have copies of enrollment information.
9. Orders all Cradle Roll materials and supplies.
10. Plans for regular meetings with nursery workers to compare information on contacts and visitation.
11. Calls in new homes, with the nursery teacher, to urge parents to enroll their child in Sunday school.
12. Helps to provide training opportunities for Cradle Roll workers.
13. Cooperates with the work of the Nursery Department.
14. Forms a Mother's Club or enlists a young couples' class as a sponsor for Cradle Roll families. Either group can give added encouragement, prayer backing, and help in making the whole church aware of the importance of Cradle Roll evangelism.

Cradle Roll Methods of Ministry

Once the Cradle Roll supervisor has been elected, the Cradle Roll ministry may begin. There are at least three distinct aspects to the ministry: (1) locating babies and families; (2) ministering to the families and their children; and (3) promoting the Cradle Roll ministry in the church.

1. Locating Babies and Families

● The supervisor should use every possible means to add names to the Cradle Roll. Solicit the help of the Avon lady, the diaper service companies, the local hospital, and the Chamber of Commerce for new arrivals in the community. Watch the local newspaper for birth announcements. Especially inquire for names of new mothers who list "no church preference" on hospital admittance cards. These names are usually available to pastors.

● Conduct an "Inside Survey." Alert every member of the church and Sunday school to help in the search for babies.

● Secure names of families with small children from reports of other visitation workers, especially those who are doing door-to-door calling.

2. Ministering to Cradle Roll Families

The ways for ministering to parents and babies are as numerous and can be as creative as the Cradle Roll workers themselves. Any means through which you can (1) show love to families, (2) help them, and (3) witness to them about Christ is a good Cradle Roll method of ministry. Here are just some of the possibilities.

Visitation. The Cradle Roll packet, *First Steps Toward God,* provides a piece of literature to leave in the home each quarter. This gives the Cradle Roll worker an opportunity to visit the baby and his family frequently. In addition, visits can be made at other times. (1) On the child's birthday take a card, a small cake, and a gift; this will endear the visitor to the child and to his parents. (2) If there is sickness in the home, the visitor should drop by to help with dishes, the wash, housecleaning, or trips to the grocery or drugstore. The visitor might also volunteer to baby-sit occasionally, so the mother can go shopping without having to take her baby along. (3) When bereavement comes, by offering sympathetic understanding, the visitor may help to save parents from bitterness and win them to Christ. In addition to calls and visits, Cradle Roll families also appreciate greeting cards or short notes from time to time.

Baby Dedication. The Cradle Roll visitor should inform parents of the opportunity to dedicate their baby to the Lord. Those who want to do so should be allowed to, regardless of their own spiritual condition. This may be the tie to win them to the church.

Special Events. Throughout the year at periodic intervals, the church can recognize the Cradle Roll homes and babies. For example, in the fall or winter, before Rally Day or Christmas, the workers could contact every Cradle Roll home personally to invite parents and children to attend. In the spring, honor Cradle Roll families on "Baby Day." The program can include such things as a baby dedication, an introduction of babies and their parents, and presentation of a small gift to each family. In the summer, consider a party for parents and Cradle Roll workers. Have a short program with light refreshments. Include the pastor and his wife and some of the young parents from the church. Provide helpers to take care of the children.

Cradle Roll Class Sponsorship Plan. An adult class, preferably a young couples' class, should be encouraged to sponsor the Cradle Roll. Doing this helps strengthen the tie between the church and Cradle Roll families. It also gives young church mothers, who have common interests with Cradle Roll mothers, opportunity to develop friendships with them. This plan helps to interest more persons in Cradle Roll work and provides additional stimulus for young couples to help with Cradle Roll visitation and outreach. Also, when parents of Cradle Roll babies attend Sunday school, this is the class that will benefit.

Under this plan, the Cradle Roll supervisor and her helpers are selected from the sponsoring class. They report to the class on their progress in finding new families and working with them. Class members, as individuals or as a group, can both minister to and socialize with the Cradle Roll families.

Mothers Club. A mothers club is a group of Cradle Roll and nursery mothers in the church who meet regularly for fellowship, study, activities, and service. The purpose of the organization is to strengthen friendships between Cradle Roll and nursery mothers, to teach parenting, and ultimately to win Cradle Roll parents to the Lord. At the club meetings, provide a variety of programs—special speakers, hobby demonstrations, service activities, and group discussions related to child care topics.

Books. Create a circulating library of good books for

parents. The Cradle Roll visitor can take these to the homes when she visits.

Greeters. When Cradle Roll parents come to church for the first time, the Cradle Roll supervisor should be on hand to greet them. She should introduce them to the nursery attendant who will care for their child.

Nursery Facilities. Do all you possibly can to provide clean and adequate nursery facilities for the Cradle Roll child when he is brought to the church. New parents are particularly anxious about their child's physical environment. A new family may be either strongly attracted to, or repelled from, a church by their nursery facilities.

3. Promoting the Cradle Roll Program

It is vitally important for the entire church to be aware of the Cradle Roll program of evangelism and outreach and to support this program in every way possible. Church members who know and care about the Cradle Roll can assist in many ways—by befriending unchurched families, by informing the church of new babies born in their communities, by praying for Cradle Roll families, and by being warm and friendly when new families begin attending church. Here are ways to keep the Cradle Roll before the church.

Wall Chart. Use the wall chart, "Our Babies," to name and picture each child in the Cradle Roll. Place this in a prominent spot in the church so that it is seen often. It is also nice to give the parents of the babies a copy of the picture of their child.

Special Events. The program events discussed earlier are an excellent way to help church members become acquainted with Cradle Roll families.

Cradle Roll Sponsorship Plan. As was discussed before, this plan helps to interest young adults in particular in the Cradle Roll ministry. Once a month, reserve a few moments for Cradle Roll visitors to report on their work and on contacts made with unchurched families. Follow this with a time of prayer for the new families.

Records. The *First Steps Toward God* packet provides a form to use to enroll children in the Cradle Roll. Make out additional copies of this form to give to the teacher or secretary of the young adult class, to the Nursery Department supervisor, and to the pastor. Also, keep records of calls made to the home and of incidents pertaining to the child and his family. This information will help interested workers keep up to date on the progress being made with the family.

It has often been said that "the baby is the key" which opens the door to the homes of unchurched young parents. Through the Cradle Roll ministry, you can use this key and win young families to the Lord.

Resources

First Steps Toward God/Cradle Roll-Nursery Packet
"Train Up a Child"/Cradle Roll Calendar
Growth Chart
How to Teach Your Children About God
"Our Babies" Chart
Life Can Have Meaning

B. Music and Drama

Participation in music and dramatic activities gives children many learning opportunities, plus the opportunity to perform for and worship with the entire congregation. Some churches organize choirs for every age level from kindergarten through junior. In recent years, along with singing, children have enjoyed putting on children's musicals, which also involve some dramatic activity. While not all children will want to participate in these ministries, they are an excellent learning experience for those who do.

Many music and drama resources are available from the Nazarene Publishing House.

C. Reading

Providing quality reading material for children in the church is a special ministry often overlooked by many children's workers. An effective reading ministry can be carried out by providing a library in the Children's Department. Or, a portion of the church library can be set aside for children's books. Arrange special times for children to use the library; encourage them to check out books and take them home. Read to children during Sunday school, children's church, and other children's meetings.

Check the Nazarene Publishing House Catalog for a variety of good children's books. The book *Honey for a Child's Heart* is an excellent text to use in selecting children's literature. And don't overlook the periodicals furnished to public school libraries. These will help you keep abreast of the latest in children's books.

D. Bible Memorization

A comprehensive plan for memorizing Bible verses is now available for kindergarten through junior ages. This is a complete revision of the old Bible Memorization Program for Children and is much more complete. The memory program has been coordinated with memorization activities in other ministries; but it can also be offered as a separate ministry to children. If you wish to use this plan, select a Bible memory director to administer the program, along with helpers he may need.

In the revised memory program, children have opportunity to memorize verses on four levels. Included as part of the program are these materials: a leader's guide, a pupil book for each age level, certificates of achievement, and honor seals.

This concludes our discussion of the various ministries available to children in the Church of the Nazarene. All of these are important, but keep always in mind that the ministry of Sunday school is the basic minimum requirement for every church; it is the foundation of any total ministry program for children. But beyond that, the church must look at the needs of its children and at the staff and resources it has available. When needs and resources have been determined, the church can then plan to add the ministries that will meet the needs of its children.

REFERENCE NOTES

1. Peter P. Person, *An Introduction to Christian Education* (Grand Rapids: Baker Book House, 1958), p. 143-45.

10

Unless the church is able to win
her boys and girls, she will die
from her own lack of efficiency!
ROBERT D. TROUTMAN

Leading a
Child to Christ

How can we help growing boys and girls know God as a real and guiding presence in their lives? There is no more urgent question facing us. In today's world, children need the security which only an intelligent faith in God can give.

When we come to a discussion of the steps in leading a child to Christ, many questions are immediately raised. Can a child really be converted? If so, at what age? What about the age of accountability? When does that occur? Don't children who early become Christians later reject their childhood experience?

As they ask these questions, workers with children recall experiences they have had with boys and girls. For example, at boys' and girls' camp one year, one little girl ran up to an adult friend and excitedly exclaimed, "I've been saved three times."

"I got saved at camp again this year," reported another. "Every year at camp I get saved."

At another camp, the director said to his staff, "Let's make it our goal to see that *every* child goes to the altar and is saved this year." As he spoke, one counsellor thought of a girl in her group who had gone to the altar in tears three nights in succession. Was this child saved or not? How should she report at the end of camp when conversion statistics were requested?

It's evident that confusion exists. Any children's worker who really loves boys and girls and wants to see them become Christians cannot help but be concerned when he hears such remarks from children or from overzealous children's workers. And yet, when we look at the weight of history, it is impossible to deny that some children can understand the significance of Christ's death for them personally and can be led to a meaningful, lasting conversion experience.

Consider these facts:

- Adam Clarke, the famous Bible commentator, was saved at age four. Isaac Watts, the hymn writer, was saved at nine.
- Out of a group of 24 students preparing for definite Christian service, 12 were converted before the age of 12 years.
- According to a study by Roy B. Zuck and Gene Getz of 3,000 Christian young people, one out of eight received Christ as Savior before the age of six. Fifty percent of those surveyed were saved during the elementary years (grades one to six).[1]

When we look at these statistics, it is clear that we should not make the mistake of treating lightly the salvation of children. In approaching children with the claims of Christ we must use care—and methods appropriate to children, not adults. But we can approach them with the confidence of knowing that children can be saved.

I recall hearing the story of a Christian mother who tells of the conversion of her son, Edward, when he was just four. One night he attended a revival service at which his father was preaching. After the invitation, the mother felt a tug at her skirts.

"Mommy, I need to go," whispered a small voice. His mother thought that Edward wanted to leave the service to go to the cabin.

"It will soon be over; then we'll go," she answered back. But that was not what the boy wanted at all. More clearly this time he indicated that he wanted to go to the altar and pray for Jesus to come into his life.

The mother, wanting to be sure he knew what he was doing, made it as difficult as possible for him to go. She explained that he would be giving his whole life to Jesus to be "Jesus' boy" from that time on. Edward agreed that that was what he wanted to do.

Finally she said, "If you go, you'll have to go alone."

Quickly Edward replied, "I will, if you'll let me out of the seat."

It took him only a few moments to pray and then to turn to his parents (who had quickly joined him) with a smile and say, "I feel good inside now." Today, Edward is in full-time Christian service. His mother is quick to state that he did not live a perfect Christian life all those years; but he never got away from the meaning of that experience.

A conversion this young is out of the ordinary and generally occurs only when the child comes from a strong two-parent Christian home. But it does point to the fact that a child's conversion can be real—and lasting. The child's experience must grow through the years; and he will probably experience spiritual ups and downs during that time. But a childhood conversion is often a stabilizing influence which helps to keep the child—and later the teen or young adult—from the paths of serious rebellion against God. Also, those who are saved as children have an entire lifetime to serve God.

There are many stories of children who made an early decision for Christ but later rejected it. Sometimes this rejection was at least partially the result of poor methods of child evangelism. In one church, the evangelist devoted his entire sermon to graphic descriptions of people who rejected Christ at a revival and then were killed on the way home from church or shortly after. Following this, and a lengthy altar call, he walked up and down the church aisles, tapping children on the shoulder and inviting them to come to the altar. In no time, the altars were lined with boys and girls who had literally been frightened into making a commitment. Perhaps some of these decisions were real and lasting; but in most cases, tactics like this produce only fear, guilt, and future problems over the meaning of the conversion experience.

Another child was told, "Unless you cry at an altar, you cannot be saved. If you were truly sorry for your sins, you would cry." Since this child had never cried at the altar, he spent years trying to be sorry for his sins and trying to be saved. Because of one worker's misinformation, this child spent years in spiritual uncertainty.

Experiences like these cause many people to feel that we should not attempt to win boys and girls to the Lord. But this is not the answer. If we refuse to present the message of salvation to children, we are, like the disciples, guilty of hindering children from coming to Jesus. Instead, we need to learn all we can about the right ways to deal with children, so that we can help them to experience a meaningful relationship with Christ.

What Is Child Evangelism?

To many in children's work, the term *evangelism* refers only to those attempts made to secure a personal commitment from the child during a children's crusade, a revival service, or an invitation given in Sunday school class. Such a commitment must be included in a definition, but to stop there is to do grave injustice to the program of child evangelism. The term might better be defined as *process*—a process in which crisis conversion is preceded by careful Christian teaching and is followed by nurture which helps the child become established in his Christian experience.

The idea of process does not in any way minimize our belief that a crisis experience is necessary. It means simply that the conversion experience is most likely to survive when it is built upon a foundation provided by sound Christian teaching and nurtured by a continued program of instruction. No child drifts into Christian experience. Christian training will do much to bring the child to the point when he realizes he needs God's forgiveness—but it can never substitute for it.

Sunday school teachers, Caravan workers, children's church leaders, and others have an especially great opportunity as they work with boys and girls. They can teach children about God and His love. They can explore the plan of salvation with them. Then, when the opportunity presents itself, the worker may lead the child to Christ. There is no greater privilege than this!

When Is a Child "Ready"?

Before a person can experience Christian conversion,

several conditions must be present in his life. First, the person must have some concept of God as a Person, one who loves him and wants his love in return. Next, the person must know the difference between right and wrong, and must be able to experience sorrow for wrongdoing. He must have at least a basic understanding of what Jesus did to make salvation possible, and what it means to trust in the Lord.

The person must also have the ability to make a rational choice. Conversion involves the emotions; but a commitment based only on emotion is unlikely to survive. The entire process of conversion/Christian living involves choosing some things and rejecting others. A person who is saved must be able to think and make these choices. And finally, in order to be really converted, the person must be moved by the Holy Spirit. It is impossible to become a Christian unless the Holy Spirit has led the individual to the point of decision.

Where do children stand in relation to these criteria for salvation? This varies widely from child to child, based on age, home environment, spiritual background, and mental and spiritual maturity. As we saw in the incident about Edward, some preschoolers have reached a point of maturity where they can make a commitment to Christ. Other children of 10, 11, and even 12 seem to lack any real awareness of their spiritual need. This difference can occur even among children in the same family who have grown up in a similar environment. One missionary mother recalled the different experiences of her six children. Aileen, the oldest child, reached a point of spiritual awakening at about age 12. Lois, her sister, was almost an adult before it dawned on her that she was a lost sinner who needed to repent. Yet several of the boys in the family were saved rather young—two of them at ages 4 and 6.

Although a child's understanding of God as a loving Person, of the differences between right and wrong, of making choices, and of the plan of salvation generally increase with chronological age, this is not consistently true for all children. An older child from an overly strict home may find it harder to relate to God as a loving Person than a younger child from a more permissive atmosphere. Some younger children have had more experiences in making choices than have others who are older. Many young children who have been raised in the church

know far more about the plan of salvation than do older children
brought in through the bus ministry.

All of this means that those working with children need to
know the general characteristics of children at various stages,
and they also need to know children personally. Detailed information about general characteristics of children is given in this
book and in each of the age-level textbooks produced by the
Department of Children's Ministries. Other information about
specific children can be gained through observation, through
experiences with the children, and through talks with their
parents and with the children themselves.

In discussing the salvation of children, Dr. Albert Harper
has suggested that nursery and kindergarten children can be
saved; primaries and middlers may be saved; and juniors ought
to be saved. However, even this is just a guideline, for at any
point in a child's experience, the Holy Spirit can quicken him,
revealing God's love, helping him experience sorrow for sin, and
helping him understand what it means to give his life to Jesus.
However, these thoughts do point us to the fact that it is
unrealistic to expect every child in any particular class or
group to become a Christian. Some are ready and some are
not.

Under pressure, children will come to the altar for a variety
of reasons—out of fear, to please adults, or out of an emotional
desire to "please Jesus." Because of this, teachers need to keep
two important principles in mind as they work with boys and
girls.

First, we must avoid rushing ahead of the Holy Spirit's
dealings with the child. Teach the facts of salvation clearly
and give opportunities to respond; but do not put undue pressure on the child. Do not plead, threaten, or make coming to
the altar like winning a contest. When we do, we subtly
motivate children to please adults or keep up with their peers.
Instead, invite the children to do something they would not
normally do. If the Holy Spirit is truly dealing with the child,
he will respond by doing what is hard for him.

Second, never reject a child's response to God, even if it
does not truly qualify as a conversion experience. Suppose, for
example, that a middler responds to an invitation but seems
only to want to pray and tell Jesus that he loves Him. By
all means, guide the child to do so. Do not label this for the

child as a conversion experience, but let him know that you are happy with his response to God. In this way, you can meet the child's current needs and keep the door open for spiritual growth and future commitment.

How can you recognize the child who probably is ready to be saved? There is no way to be absolutely certain. However, in the book *When Can a Child Believe?* Eugene Chamberlain describes some things which may indicate the child has a spiritual need for conversion. Watch for these signs.

1. The child may begin to ask a number of thoughtful questions about "being saved," "going to heaven," "my sins," "baptism," or "joining the church." Questions like these *may* indicate that the child feels the need to be saved.

2. His behavior may change drastically. Under conviction, quiet children may become rebellious or noisy. Loud children may become unusually quiet.

3. He may experience exaggerated fear—of being hurt, of doing new things, of dying, or of the Lord's second coming.

4. He may develop an increased interest in Bible study or suddenly come to dislike Sunday school and church. In the latter instance the child may not even realize why he feels this way; but subconsciously he has associated church with his feeling of conviction.[2]

Your knowledge of each child, coupled with talks with his parents and the prompting of the Holy Spirit, will help you to know when a particular child is ready to be saved. And when he is, you will want to be ready to lead him in this experience.

Preparing to Lead Children to Christ

It takes a special kind of person to help lead boys and girls to Christ. This person must be kind, loving, and one who truly wants to help meet the spiritual needs of children. He also needs to be well-informed about children, so that mistakes in working with them can be avoided. Here are some ways you can prepare yourself to be an effective child evangelist.

1. Be a committed Christian yourself. Only when you experience the reality of God in your own life can you share that reality with children. Yours is a special kind of teaching—to communicate God to children in such a way they can also experience reality with Him. You must know Christ as your own personal Savior.

2. Be sensitive to the Holy Spirit. Remember, it is the Holy Spirit who draws the child to Christ. He is the One who convicts people of their need of a Savior. You do not need to create guilt in your children. Let the Holy Spirit do His work. He will lead you when the time is right.

3. Have a plan. Know what to do if a child asks you how to become a Christian. The booklet *Really Living* is an easy-to-use tool designed to use in leading children to Christ. Copies of this booklet are available from the Nazarene Publishing House. You should always have a few copies in your Bible, ready to use at a moment's notice. Detailed instruction for using the booklet are given in the *Really Living Leader's Guide,* by Bill Young. Every children's worker should read this guide and be thoroughly familiar with its plan. You will need to adapt the plan to fit the needs of different children, but it will give you a starting point. Rely on the leadership of the Holy Spirit, but have a plan ready for Him to use if He wishes.

4. Remember that children are persons with their own wills. No matter how much you want them to be saved, only they can make their decision for Christ. A commitment that is coerced evaporates the minute the pressure is withdrawn.

5. When you give an evangelistic invitation, let your children know exactly what you want them to do. Use concrete words they can understand. An example of one approach is to tell children that they need to do three things to be saved:

Ask the Lord to forgive them.

Believe that He will.

Confess their sins. That means to tell God what they have done wrong and that they are sorry for it.

Make it as simple as *A, B, C.*

6. Let children respond to an invitation spontaneously. Wait a few moments to let the Holy Spirit speak, then gather workers for prayer. If the message has been clear, children who are ready to be saved will respond.

When a Child Responds

Here is a good procedure to follow when dealing with a child who has responded to a salvation invitation. Workers may use this plan in a classroom setting or when a child responds to an invitation in an adult worship service.

1. Gently touch the child on the arm to gain his attention. If you do not know him, ask him his name.

2. Calling him by name, ask him why he came to the altar. Be careful not to put words in the child's mouth. His answer may not be what you expected, but accept it as a genuine answer to your question. Many times children are moved to go to the altar to ask God to heal a sick relative or an injured pet, or to pray for someone they know who is not a Christian. Still others will confess that they do not know why they responded to an invitation. If this occurs, pray briefly with the child, thanking God for him or praying about the need he has expressed. Then send him back to his seat.

3. If the child expresses a spiritual need, review the plan of salvation presented in *Really Living,* or explain the "Ask, Believe, and Confess" requirements. Be brief. A simple explanation is all that is needed.

4. Use scripture to make the invitation personal. Read John 3:16 and 1 John 1:9, substituting the child's name for the personal pronouns.

5. Let the child pray. Pray *silently* along with him.

6. When the child has finished praying, ask him what God did for him. If the Lord has forgiven him, he should be able to tell you so. If the child does not know, you may repeat the information in *Really Living* to clarify any questions he might have. Ask him if he understands what the booklet says at each step along the way. Then let the child pray again. Use the written prayer only if the child has no idea how to pray on his own. Then ask the child what the Lord did for him. He should be able to answer. If there is still some question in the child's mind, he may not have been ready to seek forgiveness. Close the altar session with a prayer of thanks for the child. Let him know you are glad he responded to the invitation; but leave the door open for him to respond again at a later date, when he understands his need more fully.

7. Pray a thank-You prayer for God's work in the child's life. If the child asked for forgiveness and believes he was forgiven, thank God for this. Pray that God will help him grow into a strong Christian.

Follow Up

Once the child has accepted Jesus as Savior, his Christian

growth has just begun. He needs the guidance and counsel of mature Christians now more than ever.

If possible, begin your follow-up by going with the child as he tells his parents of his decision for Christ. This is especially important for children from non-Christian homes. Many boys and girls are afraid to tell their parents about their conversion. Your going with them will give them strength and courage. Your presence will also help the parents to respond well to the child. If you have visited in the home and built rapport with the parents, your presence at this time will do much to reduce their fears.

Give older children a copy of the booklet *Living as a Christian* (available from Nazarene Publishing House). This booklet introduces children to their Christian responsibilities and explains the meaning of baptism and other church ordinances. You may also give a copy of the booklet to the parents. Let them ask you any questions they might have. Some will think the child has now joined the church. Assure them that the child's relationship to your local congregation is unchanged. It is his relationship with God that is different. Use this opportunity to give the parents an adult tract explaining the meaning of salvation.

Tell the pastor of the child's conversion. The pastor may wish to visit in the child's home to talk with him about his decision and to answer any additional questions the family might have. This contact with the family may lead to involving the parents as well as the children in the church.

Finally, if an older child—a junior—seems mature in his faith, you may want to approach him about church membership. If enough juniors are interested, your pastor may conduct a class to prepare them to join the church. The junior age is the traditional age for joining the Nazarene church, because juniors are able to understand the basic church doctrines and standards. *This Is My Church*, by Robert D. Troutman; *Beliefs of My Church*, by Ronald F. Gray; and *It Happened at Pilot Point*, by Bill Young, are three books that can be used as texts for a junior churchmanship class. Juniors need to be trained before they are received into church membership. If there are not enough juniors for a class, the pastor may work with individual children. The boys and girls may read books at home and meet with the pastor to discuss the meaning of church membership. Once children have completed a membership training course, they should be received as church members. This is an important part of their Christian nurture.

Evangelism is one of your most important privileges and responsibilities. Kathryn Blackburn Peck has expressed it this way.

I Led a Child to Christ

Today, I led a child to Christ,
A child unfettered by earth's care,
And all unmarred by scarlet sin,
How clear and simple was his prayer!
"Forgive me, God, for wrongs I've done,
And keep me always straight and true.
I want to serve You all my life,
And do just what You'd have me do."

Today, I brought a child to Christ,
And many precious days and years
To spend in service for the King;
A life free from regretful tears—
An open mind to learn the way—
A voice that will not shun to speak
The truth—a heart to pray
And youthful zeal the lost to seek.

I thank Thee, God, for granting me
Wisdom to read upon his face
His readiness to come to Thee,
His willingness to trust Thy grace.
Whatever treausres may be mine
To keep and cherish on life's way,
None shall outshine this brightest one—
I led a CHILD to Christ today!

REFERENCE NOTES

1. Roy B. Zuck and Gene A. Getz, *Christian Youth—an In-Depth Study* (Chicago: Moody Press, 1968), p. 41.

2. Eugene Chamberlain, *When Can a Child Believe?* (Nashville: Broadman Press, 1973), pp. 50-52.

The work is too heavy for you;
you cannot handle it alone.
JETHRO, in Exod. 18:18

11

Organize for Action

- Total ministry to children—what a tremendous opportunity!
- Total ministry to children—what a tremendous lot of work!
- Total ministry to children—how can I possibly get the job done?

Were these some of your thoughts as you have read the preceding chapters describing the need for and methods of providing a total ministry to children? As local director of children's ministries, have you felt completely overwhelmed by all that needs to be done? Do you often feel that there is no way for you—one individual—to even begin to accomplish what needs to be accomplished? Have you been struggling to do so and become discouraged because you are only scratching the surface?

If so, then you are not alone in your dilemma. In fact, one of the greatest leaders in the Bible faced a similar problem as he sought to meet the needs of God's people. The leader's name was Moses. Consider his situation—and the solution that was finally suggested to him. The scene was the Sinai desert where Moses and the people were camped. Moses' father-in-law,

Jethro, had just come for a visit. The first evening, Moses and Jethro had an excellent time of sharing together all that God had done for them. But then—

> The next day Moses took his seat to serve as judge for the people, and they stood around him from morning till evening. When his father-in-law saw all that Moses was doing for the people, he said, "What is this you are doing for the people? Why do you alone sit as judge, while all these people stand around you from morning till evening?"
>
> Moses answered him, "Because the people come to me to seek God's will. . . ."
>
> Moses' father-in-law replied, "What you are doing is not good. You and these people who come to you will only wear yourselves out. The work is too heavy for you; you cannot handle it alone. Listen now to me and I will give you some advice . . . You must be the people's representative before God . . . Teach them the decrees and laws, and show them the way to live and the duties they are to perform. But select capable men from all the people—men who fear God, trustworthy men . . . and appoint them as officials over thousands, hundreds, fifties and tens. . . . That will make your load lighter, because they will share it with you. If you do this and God so commands, you will be able to stand the strain, and all these people will go home satisfied."
>
> Moses listened to his father-in-law and did everything he said.
>
> *Exod. 18:13-15, 17-24*

As we examine this episode from Moses' life, several important principles related to ministry appear. First, we see that it is common for leaders to attempt to do too much. Part of the reason for this is that when a person takes on a new responsibility, he is not immediately aware of all the details of the job. Once involved, these details begin to surface; but the leader, rather than stepping back, taking a new look at the job, and delegating some responsibilities, tends to assume additional duties as they arise. This goes on until all of a sudden he—or someone else—is overwhelmed by the fact that his job is simply too big.

Second, this incident points out the problems that arise when one person does attempt too much. Both he and those he is trying to serve suffer. Not only was Moses in great danger of breaking down under the strain of the work, but the people were not being helped as quickly as they should have been. What is more, because Moses failed to involve others in the work, he was neglecting one of the primary tasks of an administrator—to tap human resources and help develop them to their full potential. He was not allowing others in his group to reap the rewards which come from serving others.

Jethro's solution to the problem was simply to organize for more effective ministry, and to work through that organization. By working with and through others, rather than trying to do everything for himself, Moses would (1) better meet the needs of people; (2) involve others in ministry; and (3) free himself to do those things which were most vital for him—the top administrator—to do. Working through an organization in no way lessened Moses' responsibilities. Notice that he was to continue to be a leadership model for his helpers—and the people—and that he had important tasks of his own. What organization did was to allow Moses to be the best possible leader for everyone concerned.

These principles need to be applied to the work of children's ministry today. As director of children's ministries, you have important responsibilities. There are things that only you can do; but like Moses, you also need an organization through which and with which you can work to provide total ministry to children. That organization has been provided for you in the new structure of the children's division. It is the Children's Council. This council is made up of representatives from each of the church's ministries to children. Its responsibility is to work with the children's director to plan and to make provision for all the work that is done in children's ministries.

With this in mind, let us take a look at your responsibilities as children's director, and then at the way you can work with the council to provide an effective total ministry to children.

The Local Director of Children's Ministries

In accordance with the *Manual,* the local director of children's ministries is nominated by the Board of Christian Life, with approval of the pastor, and elected by the Church Board. Once elected, the local director becomes an ex officio member of the Board of Christian Life. This position allows him to coordinate the work of children's ministries with that of youth and adult.

The task of the local director is to coordinate a program of total ministry to children—Sunday, weekday, annual, and special. Notice the word *coordinate*. This points out that the local director's responsibilities center mainly in planning and working through others—not carrying out of the various ministries. For this reason, the person elected as local director needs to be someone with strong administrative abilities and the ability to work harmoniously with adults. Often a church elects someone who is "wonderful with children," but who may not be a good leader and administrator. The director of children's ministries should be someone who is interested in children, and probably someone who has worked with them. But just as important are the abilities to plan, organize, delegate, and work with adults.

The responsibilities of the local director can be categorized as follows:

1. **Children's Council**
   a. Constructs meeting agenda for the Children's Council and chairs all council meetings.
   b. Meshes calendar items with the Children's Council calendar and communicates to all workers involved.
   c. Coordinates mission and stewardship education through the Children's Council.
   d. Evaluates the total ministry to children through the Children's Council.

2. **Sunday School**
   a. Serves as Sunday school superintendent of the children's department.
   b. Submits a monthly Sunday school report to the Christian Life chairman.
   c. Recommends to the Board of Christian Life supplemental curriculum items and resources to be used.

3. **Personnel and Budget**
   a. Recommends an asking budget to the Board of Christian Life; dispenses monies according to the priorities of the children's division.
   b. Nominates teachers and workers for children's ministries (in consultation with the pastor and the chairman of the Board of Christian Life) to the Board of Christian Life.
   c. Provides for the training of teachers and leaders in the children's division.

4. Records and Reports

    a. Receives all reports and is responsible for department records. In addition to the Sunday school records, the local director is responsible to see that records are kept for Caravan, Cradle Roll, VBS, and other children's ministries.

    b. Reports regularly to the Board of Christian Life the activities of children's ministries.

The Children's Council

Every church, no matter what the size, should have a Children's Council. In a small church this may consist of only two people planning for children's ministries—a children's director who is also a Sunday school teacher, and a second teacher from a different children's department. In larger churches, the size of the council grows as ministries are added. However, the need for the council and the work that it does remains the same whether the church has a membership of 50 or 5,000.

The council is comprised of representatives from each of the ministries for children which the church provides. Since the *Manual* does not stipulate consistent procedures for selecting these representatives, it is suggested that they be nominated by the children's director, approved by the pastor, and elected by the Board of Christian Life. The following chart shows the makeup of a council in a church which is implementing most of the ministries available for children. In a smaller church, there will be fewer representatives, because fewer ministries are provided. Also, in some' situations the same person represents more than one ministry on the council. The children's church director, for example, may also be in charge of mission education. In a larger church, there may be more representatives if the Sunday school has one person from each age-level department. Additional representatives may be added if your church provides these ministries: music, drama, reading, Bible memorization, special activities days, training, and outreach.

The Children's Council in Action. To gain a better understanding of the way in which a Children's Council works, let's drop in on a typical meeting of the council at First Church of the Nazarene, Anytown, U.S.A.

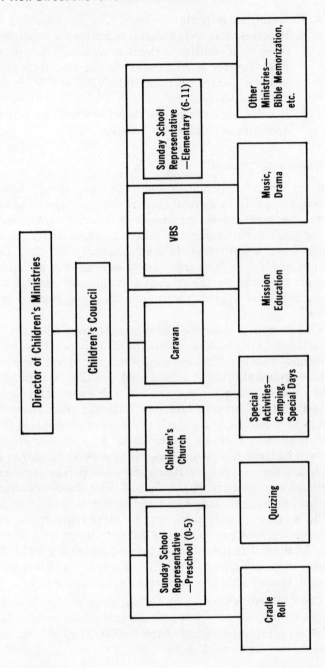

Tom Taylor, the children's director, opens the meeting with prayer and a brief devotional. Then he calls on Marge Smith to share with the group the way the Lord answered prayer in her children's church. For several months, she had been short two staff members and could not seem to find anyone with the burden to help in this ministry. Then the Adams family joined the church and, in just a few weeks, *volunteered* to help. Marge reports enthusiastically that they have already endeared themselves to the children and are doing a wonderful job. Everyone in the group is thrilled with this report, for in recent meetings they had prayed with Marge about the need for workers.

Next, Tom presents a report from the Board of Christian Life. They have approved the council's recommendation—made in the previous meeting—that VBS be held during the last two weeks of June. Finances for the school have also been determined. Anne Carter, the VBS director, reports that she has ordered a sample kit of literature and is beginning to make plans for the school.

After a few more announcements of this type, Tom opens the meeting up for new business. Immediately the Kellys, who are in charge of mission education, ask for the council's help in planning for a spring Mission Jamboree for the children. They would like to hold the Jamboree on Saturday, May 14, and they would also like input from the council on some good activities to include in the program.

Ted Bailey, Caravan director, objects to the date suggested; it is the same day as the district Caravan Fair. After discussion it is agreed that it would not be good to have two major events on the same day, since most children are involved in both Caravan and mission education. A look at the children's calendar of events helps the group to settle tentatively on Saturday, May 28. Tom assures the Kellys that he will clear this date immediately with the Board of Christian Life.

The council now turns its attention to helping the Kellys think of resource persons and activities for the Jamboree. Nancy White, middler supervisor, reminds them that the Coxes, who are retired missionaries to India, live on the district. Perhaps they could be brought in as special guests. Mrs. Cox could fix some Indian food for the children to sample. No doubt they would also have interesting curios, and perhaps slides of the country. Bill Peters, camp director, suggests that perhaps the children could work together to construct an African hut or some other type of native home. And so it goes —each member of the council making suggestions for activities and for promotion of the event. When they finish, the Kellys are really excited about the possibilities for the day.

Tom now directs the council's attention to the Sunday school statistics for the past six months. Although there is no significant drop, attendance has been lower in some departments and has leveled off in others. Tom believes that a Sunday school attendance campaign might be the answer, and he wants the council's help in planning for this. It is the consensus that if a campaign is held, it must not be so involved and complicated that valuable teaching time is lost. With this goal in mind, Tom encourages the group to think of other goals and priorities. He lists these on the chalkboard as the group discusses.

When this discussion is completed, Tom looks at his watch—it is 10 minutes to nine. He has promised the group that they will be done by nine; so with a few concluding remarks about some things they will be discussing next month, he concludes the meeting and dismisses the group.

The Work of the Children's Council. As we have seen from this example, the task of the Children's Council is to plan all ministry to children—and then to make provision for the implementation of those plans. To carry out this responsibility, the council:

- Plans what ministries or activities should be made available for children, and makes recommendations to the Board of Christian Life regarding these.
- Plans how finances will be used in carrying out ministry programs and activities.
- Plans for leadership training of workers.
- Coordinates the calendar of children's ministries and events, so there is no conflict in scheduled events.
- Works together to plan various ministry events; coordinates the efforts of each ministry with others provided for children.
- Coordinates mission and stewardship education for children with the NWMS and the church board.

- Evaluates the total ministry program for children to see if it is meeting the needs of those whom it serves.

All recommendations made by the council go to the Board of Christian Life for approval. This helps to coordinate the ministries for children with those of the youth and adult divisions of the church. Once approval has been secured from the board, the plans are brought back to the Children's Council for implementation by those who are in charge of the ministries involved. For example, when Tom Taylor's group received word that the VBS dates had been approved, the VBS director was then ready to begin her work for VBS.

It is easy to see the benefits which result when a Children's Council is properly utilized.

- Communication in the Division of Children's Ministries is improved. Each area of ministry knows what is happening in other areas. No longer are the personnel of one area working against, or in competition with, those in other areas. Duplication of effort—or neglect of certain areas—can be eliminated.

- Each ministry has at its disposal the collective input of those who are involved in other ministries. The result is better planning and more creative ideas.

- The work of each person—and of the director—is reduced when all work together.

- A sense of unity is achieved.

When we see the many benefits of working through a Children's Council, it is hard to understand why anyone would attempt to direct the work of children's ministries without the aid of one. Yet there are many children's directors who, like Moses, are trying to carry the load alone. For their sakes, and for the sakes of those to whom they are trying to minister, they need to heed the advice of Jethro, who, if he were here today, would say, "Form a council of capable workers in your church—workers who fear God; for if you do this, it will make your load lighter, because they will share it with you."

These were his gifts: some to be
apostles, some prophets, some evan-
gelists, some pastors and teachers, to
equip God's people for work in his
service, to the building up of the body
of Christ.

Eph. 4:11-12, NEB

Equipping Workers for Ministry

In Chapter 11, we emphasized the fact that it is *not* the task of the local director of children's ministries to carry out all of the work of ministering to children. In order for ministry to be effective, this work should be planned and organized through a Children's Council, then implemented by all of the workers in the various areas of ministry. However, this in no way negates the importance of your task as a children's director. Though you work less directly with boys and girls, you are important as the leader, and helper of their leaders.

Take another look at the verses from Eph. 4:11-12. In them, Paul gives us "the foundation for a dynamic Bible teaching program." In addition:

> This principle, so vital to the overall ministry of the church, also applies to the work of the . . . leader. It says to you that your primary energies must be directed toward those who serve with you. Those of us who have tried to build the teaching ministry around ourselves will find a new freedom in this principle. Those of us who have not understood why there must be such an emphasis on training others will discover in Paul's teaching a beautiful truth.

> Paul is saying that we must devote ourselves to equipping our people to accomplish God's will. . . . This does not mean that we equip others so we will be free from their work;

it does not suggest that we divorce ourselves from . . . departments and classes. It does mean that the leader of God's people must be deeply involved in helping other persons grow.

When this principle is applied to your work . . . your ministry can be compounded. You will see your fellow workers accomplishing far more in God's kingdom work than you ever dreamed possible.[1]

Your major task as children's director, then, is to help those who work under you to do an effective job of reaching and teaching boys and girls through the ministries in which they work. There are two ways you can do this: (1) by understanding children and children's work; and (2) by using every means possible to train, equip, and support workers in their tasks.

Understand Children and Children's Work

To be a helpful and supportive leader of those who are actively involved in teaching children, you need to know at least the basics about children of all ages, and of the ministries provided for them. Possessing this basic knowledge helps you first as you guide workers to plan for children—choosing equipment, supplies, and methods of teaching. Second, it gives you a better foundation of understanding when workers share with you their successes, or their needs and frustrations.

You can gain this knowledge about children and children's work in a variety of ways. First of all, read. This book is a beginning; but there are many others which will help you. As the children's director, you should read each of the age-group texts for Sunday school workers, plus the guidebooks for each ministry. *Vacation Bible School: A Creative Summer Ministry,* by Jeannette Wienecke, is an example of this. The other books listed at the end of this text are also good. In addition, occasionally look through the curriculum materials for Sunday school and other ministries. Note changes, improvements, and the information they present on working with children.

Another way to gain basic knowledge you need is to observe children and keep in contact with them. Occasionally visit Sunday school classes and other organizations. Observe what the children do and say. In odd moments, talk to children. One children's director made it her habit to visit personally with at least three children each Sunday. She arrived early enough to greet the early comers. When she saw children in the hall, she stopped and spoke briefly with them. This not only taught her about children and helped her feel close to them, but it also helped the children learn to know and like her as a person.

For further helpful information, attend workshops and conferences on your district or in nearby areas. All of these will gradually build up your store of knowledge about children and children's work.

Equipping Workers for the Task

Many of the people in your church who work with boys and girls will be untrained for their work. A few may be, or have been, public school teachers, but the majority are housewives, businessmen, and professional people. Some may even be teens or young adults in college. While some of these people may be very skilled in their occupation, this does not necessarily mean they understand children or know how to work with them.

For this reason, as the children's director, you must invest a great deal of your time in training workers for their task. This process begins the moment you recruit someone to take a position; it continues as long as the person works with you in children's ministries.

Your task of training workers falls into several large categories: (1) enlisting them for the task; (2) training them to do the task; (3) supporting them in their work; and (4) evaluating their work as the basis for further equipping efforts.

Enlisting Workers

"Jim! Oh, Jim," called out Children's Director Paul Davidson as he dashed down the hall. "May I see you a moment?"

Jim Blakely, on his way home from church, paused and waited for Paul to catch up. A few moments later, he wished he could have ignored the urgent call. For there in Paul's hand was a junior teacher's quarterly.

"Jim," Paul said breathlessly, "we need a teacher for the junior boys. The Petersons just quit. Do you think you might be able to take on this responsibility?"

"Well, I—" began Jim, but he got no further.

"It's really not that bad a job," continued Paul. "You just meet with the class once a week, and maybe once a year for a party or something. All the lesson plans are in the quarterly, and we'll get you any supplies you need. What do you say? Those boys need a man teacher, you know—someone they can really look up to."

"But I—" started Jim again, but again he was stopped.

"Don't worry about missing your adult class, either," added Paul. "You can still go to their parties and all that. We really need you, Jim, so what do you say? Here, take this material and look it over. I think you'll agree that there's really nothing to teaching—especially boys. You'll have them eating out of your hand." And with that, Paul hurried down the hall to catch the pastor for a moment's conversation.

Have you ever been recruited in this fashion—or seen it happen this way? Hopefully not; but probably so. This is unfortunate, for the first step in equipping a worker to do his task well is to recruit him properly. Good recruitment techniques are important because they set the tone for the person's entire experience in ministry. When an individual is recruited to work in children's ministries, he needs to know exactly the nature of the job he is being asked to do, and the reasons why he has been considered for the responsibility. He also needs to know that those recruiting him have prayed about the situation —not just grabbed the first person who passed by. And, most of all, he needs time to think and pray before taking the assignment.

Not every person is called of God to teach children. When we read scriptures like Rom. 12:7 or 1 Cor. 12:28, we see that teaching is a spiritual gift, not an ability that everyone possesses. Furthermore, as we saw in Chapter 2, it is a serious matter to teach impressionable children. Those who do must be willing to invest their time and must live out before the children the truths they are teaching.

For these reasons, workers must be recruited in such a way that the wrong person is not placed in a job. As you recruit workers, keep these guidelines in mind.

1. Pray about the matter. When you have a position to fill, ask God to bring to your mind the names of those who might be qualified to fill it. As people come to your mind, pray about them before making the first contact. After you have talked to a candidate, pray for and with him as he gives the matter consideration.

2. Inform the worker fully of what will be expected of him

in the job you are asking him to take. Many leaders make the mistake of minimizing the job, thinking that if the person really knows what is involved, he will turn it down. This approach is wrong on two counts. First, if a person takes the job, he will soon discover exactly how much is involved. If he was not told beforehand, he will resent this and perhaps resign as soon as possible. Second, minimizing the job gives the worker a low concept of ministry; it almost invites him to do a lackadaisical job.

For these reasons, it is imperative that you be frank with those you are recruiting. This keeps the worker from becoming disillusioned or overwhelmed later on; and it also helps him to sense that children's ministry calls for some real commitment of time, talent, and spiritual resources. We do not want workers who are willing only to squeeze in ministry when there is time; we want those who take the job seriously and who will make sacrifices when they are necessary.

To help workers know what is expected, give them written job descriptions. Examples are given in this book and in other children's ministries texts. Also give workers samples of the literature and materials they will be using. Take enough time to briefly go through the materials with them. Later, if the person accepts the job, you can give more in-depth training.

3. Give the worker time to think and pray for himself. Never force a person to accept a responsibility on the spot. Because the person is committing himself to ministry—not just a trivial job—he needs time to ascertain that this really is the Lord's will for him. Assure the person that you will pray with him as he weighs the issues and decides.

4. Accept whatever decision the candidate makes. It may not be the decision you wanted, or one that you feel is right; but it is his decision and should be respected as such. Do not make the person feel guilty for turning the job down, or suggest that he is an uncommitted Christian. You can pray that he will change his mind; but in the meantime, also be looking elsewhere for someone else.

Training Workers

There are many different ways you can train workers for their task, and each method has its own benefits. For best results in training, use a variety of methods.

Be a Resource Person

As director, you can do a lot personally to help your workers. Be on the lookout for helpful magazine articles they can read. Apportion part of your children's ministries budget for the purchase of Christian education books to circulate among your workers to read. When you are the only one from your church to go to a workshop or conference, take careful notes so you can share new insights with your workers. As you read the materials in *Kaleidoscope,* distribute to the workers the information that is of particular value to them. Many directors order two sets of *Kaleidoscope* materials each quarter—one set to keep in the permanent file, the other to cut up and distribute among workers.

Above all, be a good listener. Let workers know they can feel free to come to you for help and guidance. From your background of experience with children, share ideas that have worked well for you.

Provide In-service Training

One of the best ways for a person to learn to work with children is to receive one-to-one training from a more skilled person in the field. Through this method, the novice can learn through observation, through conversation, and through practice experience. In one church there was a vacancy in the nursery twos and threes class. One lady in the church was a skilled nursery worker; but she was not able at that time to make a long-term commitment to teach. So the children's director asked her to train a willing but totally inexperienced woman for this work. For one quarter, the experienced teacher worked Sunday by Sunday with the trainee. At first, she did most of the work; but each Sunday, she relinquished a little more responsibility to her helper. By the end of the quarter, the new teacher felt confident and ready to take over. Within another quarter, she too was ready to give in-service training to another. Soon the church had two confident and excellent nursery teachers, all because of in-service training.

The promise of in-service training is often a real drawing card when you are trying to recruit workers. Many people feel a desire to help but recognize their lack of ability or experience. If they know they will get step-by-step training from someone who knows what he is doing, they do not feel so frightened to commit themselves to children's work.

Train Through Workers' Meetings

The subject of workers' meetings is one that is hotly debated in various circles. Some people advocate a weekly meeting; others declare that there is too little time and that in general the meetings are wasted effort. There is no one right answer about the number or kind of meetings you provide for workers; but workers do need some training and work sessions together. Beyond this, they should be encouraged to meet as often as necessary to get the job done efficiently.

Where only two people work together in a class or ministry, much planning can be done by telephone, or during brief periods before and after class sessions. When there are three or more workers, a monthly meeting is usually helpful.

One common complaint about workers' meetings is that they are a waste of time. This complaint is not unfounded. For example, every meeting should include a time of inspiration and challenge to workers; but some meetings contain little more than this. Workers are urged to be "enthusiastic," and to "do your best for the Lord"; but they are given few specifics about how to accomplish these goals. In other situations, too much time is wasted on chitchat and "administrivia." Workers really resent a meeting that seems to just go on and on.

To avoid these problems, a good quarterly workers' meeting should include these elements: inspiration, information, and departmental planning sessions.

Inspiration. During this portion of the meeting, present a *brief* Bible study or devotional, or ask workers (before the meeting) to share some exciting things that have happened recently in their areas of ministry. Conclude the inspiration time with prayer, taking requests from workers. Praying together over the needs of children's ministries is an effective way to build unity among workers. To make this time even more personal, occasionally break into groups of three or four. Ask each one in each group to share a request; then have each person take one request (other than his own) and pray specifically for it.

Information. This part of the session should have two parts. First, make all necessary announcements about future plans and events. If desired, get group input on important ideas and issues. Following this, present a definite training feature of general interest to all. Vary your method of presentation from time to time, using audiovisuals, special speakers, displays, demonstrations, or learning centers.

Departmental Planning. During this segment of the meeting, workers should meet together by departments or ministries to make specific plans for their work. In such a meeting they may:

▷ Set department goals.
▷ Plan ways to accomplish these goals.
▷ Consider the needs of the boys and girls in the department or ministry.
▷ Preview curriculum materials.
▷ Examine teaching suggestions in the curriculum materials.
▷ Decide on materials and supplies needed for teaching.
▷ Examine attendance patterns and make plans for improving attendance.
▷ Develop teaching plans for a unit of study.
▷ Develop plans for a Sunday teaching session.
▷ Talk about needs for new workers and replacement of workers.
▷ Discuss equipment needs.
▷ Talk about behavior problems.
▷ Plan special department activities—social events, field trips.
▷ Plan ways the department can participate in church-wide emphases.
▷ Explore teaching methods.
▷ Encourage one another.
▷ Pray.

It's easy to see that a meeting like this will be of real value to all who attend. When you provide such meetings for your workers—and are careful to begin and end them on time—you will find it much easier to encourage their faithful attendance.

Encourage Additional Types of Leadership Training

To further equip workers for their task, make every effort to involve them in training classes, and encourage them to attend district and other leadership-training conferences. Watch for information about training opportunities available in your district or area.

Encourage and Support Workers

One of the most important things you can do as a children's director is to encourage and support your workers. They need to know that you care about them as persons—not just workers in a particular field of ministry. Through personal notes or calls, let them know how much you appreciate them; and that you are available to counsel or to help as needed. When you know that a worker is facing a personal crisis—sickness in the family, for example—support him with your prayers and with other help if possible. Praise your workers to the pastor and to the congregation. One good way to do this is through the church newsletter. An occasional, brief write-up about achievements in children's ministries will do much to encourage those who are working faithfully in various areas.

It is important for workers to know that you support them in their actions. After you have made plans through the Children's Council, back up your leaders when plans are put into operation. Some actions may be unpopular with some people; if so, you need to stand solidly behind those who are trying to put into effect the things your council has decided. Be a good listener when people come to you with complaints; but in the remarks you make, always support your workers. If there is a problem that needs to be corrected, talk about it individually with the person involved. Do not create problems among workers by failure to support those who work directly with you.

The need to provide adequate training and support of children's ministries workers cannot be overestimated. Jesus spent three years training 12 men to take the gospel to the world. Without this training, it is difficult to conceive of what the disciples would have done after Jesus returned to heaven. As a children's director you cannot live and work with your staff in the intensely personal way that Jesus did with His followers; but training must not be neglected. Only when workers are trained can they even begin to minister effectively to the spiritual needs of children.

And Now What?

It is with mixed feelings that I bring to a close this chapter —and this text—on total ministry to children. As I look back over the pages, I wonder, "Did I say what needed to be said? Have I included the specific guidance that children's directors and pastors in the Church of the Nazarene need to have in order to organize and administer the work of children's ministries? But most of all, have I somehow helped you catch a glimpse of the task and the opportunity we have as we work with boys and girls?"

Recently at my church, our pastor shared the story of Steve, an eight-year-old retarded child. As he grew older, his retardation became more evident, and his concerned teacher feared that others in the class would begin to make fun of him. One Sunday, near Easter, the teacher gave each of the eight members of the class a plastic egg. She asked each pupil to put inside his or her egg something that represented new life. Because she was afraid that Steve would not understand the assignment, she told the pupils to leave their eggs unmarked and to simply place them on her desk. Then, one by one she began to open them.

The first egg contained a pretty flower. Excitedly, a little girl piped up, "I brought that one." The next egg contained a rock. Steve must have done this, thought the teacher, for a rock cannot represent new life. But no, another child waved his hand and said, "See, my rock has moss on it—it stands for new life."

When the teacher opened the third egg, she saw to her dismay that it was empty. This is Steve's, she thought, and hurriedly she set it aside to avoid embarrassing him. But this time Steve raised his hand. "Teacher, don't leave mine out," he pleaded.

"But yours is empty, Steve," said the teacher.

"I know," replied Steve. "That's because Jesus' tomb was empty, too. It stood for new life for all of us."

A few months later, Steve's physical condition deteriorated and he died. On his casket at the funeral lay eight opened plastic eggs—all empty.

As I listened to this story, I wondered: Suppose that Steve had never had the opportunity to attend Sunday school or church, or had not experienced the warm love of a concerned, caring teacher and class. Suppose that the others in Steve's class had not been able to share in the spiritual insight of this retarded child. Certainly many people's lives would have been made poorer by this loss. And yet, this incident could not have taken place had there not been a pastor, a children's director, and teachers who were willing to obey Jesus' command to "Let the . . . children come" (Matt. 19:14).

And so, as I close this chapter and book, I close it with a prayer for each of you who is involved in children's ministries in the Church of the Nazarene. Your task is not glamorous or easy. It calls for commitment, dedication, and plenty of hard work. But our church is full of dedicated people who love children, people who will make the sacrifices necessary to minister to them. I am confident that God can use each of us—at headquarters, on the district, and in local churches—to bring children into the kingdom of God!

REFERENCE NOTES

1. Mavis Allen and Max Caldwell, *Helping Teachers Teach* (Nashville: Convention Press, 1976), pp. 21-22.

Chapter Heading Quotes

1. RABBINDRANATH TAGORE in *Stray Birds*

4. WILLIAM BARCLAY, *To Train Up a Child* (Philadelphia: The Westminster Press, 1959), p. 45.

5. CORDELIA GOBUIYAN, "Dear Teacher," *Baptist Leader,* October, 1971, p. 57. Published by the American Baptist Board of Education and Publication. Used by permission.

7. CLEMENT OF ROME as cited in William Barclay, *To Train Up a Child* (Philadelphia: The Westminster Press, 1959), p. 45.

10. The *Edge,* JJA, 1975, "Christian Nurture or Crisis Experience," Robert Troutman, pp. 8-9. Published by Nazarene Publishing House. Used by permission.

Bibliography

Preschool:

BAILEY, ETHEL WESTMARK. *Teaching That Makes a Difference for Kindergarten Children.* Kansas City: Beacon Hill Press of Kansas City, 1980.

BARBOUR, MARY A. *You Can Teach 2s and 3s.* Wheaton, Ill.: Victor Books, 1974.

GILLILAND, ANNE HITCHCOCK. *Understanding Preschoolers.* Nashville: Convention Press, 1969.

HANCOCK, MAXINE. *People in Process.* Old Tappan, N.J.: Fleming H. Revell Co., 1978.

HEARN, FLORENCE CONNER. *Guiding Preschoolers.* Nashville: Convention Press, 1969.

LATHAM, JOY. *Living and Learning with Nursery Children.* Kansas City: Beacon Hill Press of Kansas City, 1977.

LINAM, GAIL. *Teaching Preschoolers.* Nashville: Convention Press, 1977.

McDANIEL, ELSIEBETH, AND RICHARDS, LAWRENCE O. *You and Preschoolers.* Chicago: Moody Press, 1975.

Elementary Children:

BAILEY, ETHEL WESTMARK. *The Ministry of Music with Children.* Kansas City: Beacon Hill Press of Kansas City, 1977.

BLACKWELL, MURIEL, AND RIVES, ELSIE. *Teaching Children in the Sunday School.* Nashville: Convention Press, 1976.

FILLMORE, DONNA. *Let's Teach with Bible Games.* Kansas City: Beacon Hill Press of Kansas City, 1977.

———. *Reaching and Teaching Middlers.* Kansas City: Beacon Hill Press of Kansas City, 1980.

ILG, FRANCES L., AND AMES, LOUISE BATES. *Child Behavior.* New York: Harper and Row, 1955.

JONES, ELIZABETH. *Teaching Primaries Today.* Kansas City: Beacon Hill Press of Kansas City, 1974.

———. *When We Share the Bible with Children.* Kansas City: Beacon Hill Press of Kansas City, 1977.

McDANIEL, ELSIEBETH. *You and Children.* Chicago: Moody Press, 1973.

RIVES, ELSIE, AND SHARP, MARGARET. *Guiding Children.* Nashville: Convention Press, 1969.

STITH, MARJORIE. *Understanding Children.* Nashville: Convention Press, 1969.

YORK, MARK A. *You CAN Teach Juniors.* Kansas City: Beacon Hill Press of Kansas City, 1980.

General:

ALLEN, MAVIS, AND CALDWELL, MAX. *Helping Teachers Teach.* Nashville: Convention Press, 1976.

BOWES, BETTY. *The Ministry of the Cradle Roll.* Kansas City: Beacon Hill Press of Kansas City, 1970.

CHAMBERLAIN, EUGENE. *When Can a Child Believe?* Nashville: Broadman Press, 1973.

DOBSON, JAMES. *Hide or Seek.* Old Tappan, N.J.: Fleming H. Revell Co., 1971.

DRESCHER, JOHN M. *Seven Things Children Need.* Scottdale, Pa.: Herald Press, 1976.

HAKES, J. EDWARD. *An Introduction to Evangelical Christian Education.* Chicago: Moody Press, 1964.

JONES, ELIZABETH. *Let the Children Come,* Kansas City: Beacon Hill Press of Kansas City, 1978.

LEBAR, LOIS. *Education That Is Christian.* Old Tappan, N.J.: Fleming H. Revell Co., 1958.

LEBAR, MARY. *Children Can Worship.* Wheaton, Ill.: Victor Books, 1976.

MEIER, PAUL D. *Christian Child-Rearing and Personality Development.* Grand Rapids: Baker Book House, 1977.

SIZEMORE, JOHN T. *Rejoice, You're a Sunday School Teacher.* Nashville: Broadman Press, 1977.

STRAUSS, RICHARD L. *Confident Children and How They Grow.* Wheaton, Ill.: Tyndale House Publishers, 1976.

YOUNG, BILL. *The Caravan Ministry.* Kansas City: Nazarene Publishing House, 1976.